MATHEMATICAL
PUZZLES

MATHEMATICAL PUZZLES OF

SAM LOYD

Selected and Edited by

MARTIN GARDNER

VOLUME TWO

Dover Publications, Inc., New York, New York

Manufactured in the United States of America

Dover Publications, Inc.
180 Varick Street
New York 14, N. Y.

CLASSIFIED TABLE OF CONTENTS

Arithmetic and Algebraic Problems

Speed and Distance Problems

Clock Problems

Game Theory Problems

Operations Research Problems

Plane Geometry Problems

Geometrical Dissection Problems

Route, Tracing, and Topological Problems

Counter and Sliding Block Problems

Solid Geometry Problems

Physics and Calculus Problems

INTRODUCTION

This is the second and final collection of mathematical puzzles taken from Sam Loyd's mammoth *Cyclopedia of Puzzles*, edited by his son and published posthumously in 1914. The two collections by no means exhaust all of Loyd's mathematical gems, but they do contain, I believe, the cream of his incredible output, and in any case, there is not a sufficient number of such puzzles left in the *Cyclopedia* to justify a third collection. As before, the text has been heavily edited to make it clearer and more accurate, but in such a way as to preserve the flavor of Loyd's style. Occasional remarks of my own will be found in brackets.

I would like to call the reader's attention to the high quality of many of Loyd's algebraic problems that lack accompanying pictures. In the *Cyclopedia* most of these puzzles have humorous illustrations, but the pictures are not essential to the text and they have been left out here in order to make room for as many short problems as possible. Among these problems, those that deal with speeds and distances are particularly difficult, and I recommend them to all students of mathematics who hope to master the calculus. Before one goes on to questions involving nonuniform rates, it is certainly necessary to be able to think clearly about uniform rates, and Loyd's challenging problems of this type are excellent training exercises–provided, of course, one tries to solve them without peeking at the answers!

I wish to thank the many readers whose letters have helped in correcting errors in the early printings of my first Loyd collection, and to express my gratitude for letters to come that will help clear the mistakes from this second volume.

March, 1960

Martin Gardner

PUZZLES

1 *What happens to the weight?*

THIS QUAINT problem in mechanics, despite its apparent
simplicity, is said to have caused Lewis Carroll considerable
disquietude. Whether the famous author of *Alice's Adventures
in Wonderland*, who was an Oxford professor of mathematics,
originated the problem is not known; but in an evil hour he
asked for information on the following:

If to a rope, passed over a frictionless pulley, is suspended a
ten-pound weight that exactly balances a monkey at the other
end, what happens to the weight if the monkey attempts to
climb the rope?

"It is very curious," Carroll wrote, "[to note] the different
views taken by good mathematicians. Price says the weight
goes *up* [with] increasing velocity. Clifton (and Harcourt)
that it goes *up* at the same rate as the monkey, while Sampson
says that it goes *down!*"

A distinguished mechanical engineer says "it would have no
more effect than a fly crawling up a rope," while a scientist

claims that "the weight would rise or lower according to the inverse ratio of the speed with which the monkey ate the apple," from which, however, should be extracted the square root of the monkey's tail. Seriously speaking, it is a pretty problem worthy of serious consideration, and one which illustrates the intimate relationship between puzzles and mechanical problems.

[To make the problem more precise, assume that both rope and wheel are weightless and frictionless.—M.G.]

2 The Hammock Puzzle.

You ARE looking down on a crudely constructed hammock. What is the least number of cords that must be cut, starting at the top and cutting toward the bottom, that will divide the hammock into two separate parts? Cuts must pass through cord segments; no cuts through intersection points are permitted.

3 The Price of Eggs

"I PAID twelve cents for the eggs I bought from the grocer," explained the cook, "but I made him throw in two extra eggs because they were so little. That made the lot cost just one cent per dozen less than the first asking price."

How many eggs did the cook buy?

4 *Solve Beppo's problems.*

HISTORY TELLS us that Euclid once tried to explain how to subdivide a circle to King Ptolemy. He was interrupted by the irate monarch exclaiming, "I am wearied by such dull lessons, and refuse to burden my memory with stupid rules!"

The great mathematician replied: "Then your majesty will graciously permit me to resign the position of Imperial Instructor, for none but a fool knows of a Royal Road to Mathematics."

"Right you are, Euc!" interjected Beppo, the court jester, as he pushed his way to the blackboard. "And in accepting the position so gracefully tendered, I will proceed to demonstrate how the great principles of mathematics can be taught by simple kindergarten methods which children can understand and remember.

"Philosophers say that what is learned with pleasure is never forgotten, but knowledge cannot be beaten into the head with a wormwood club. Pupils should not be made to commit rules to memory. Everything should be explained so that they can formulate rules in their own language. A pedagogue who teaches rules would be a good teacher of parrots!

"With the kind permission of your majesty, I will now elucidate the subdivision of the circle by asking Tommy Riddles, the court crier, to show into how many pieces it is possible to divide a pancake with seven straight cuts of a knife.

"Furthermore, to add a point to the moral of the story of the sword of Damocles, which is shown to be suspended over our heads by a single thread, we will proceed to impress it indelibly upon the memory by asking: 'Why is the blade of that sword curved?'

"Noting with pleasure the presence of a diagram of my distinguished predecessor's famous forty-seventh proposition, which proves that the square of the hypotenuse is equal to the sum of the squares on the other two sides, I will ask the author of this proposition to tell us how many rails of equal length would be required to enclose a right-angled triangular field if one of the three sides was forty-seven rails long?" [That is, find a right-triangle of integral sides, one side of which is forty-seven.—M.G.]

The clown's forty-seventh proposition will doubtless prove that many good mathematicians have much yet to learn regarding the wonderful principles of the Pythagorean theorem.

5 *Conscientious Milkman*

IT WAS the daily practice of a conscientious milkman to fill his two sixteen-gallon cans with pure milk before he started out to serve customers on four different streets, the same number of quarts being delivered on each street.

After serving the first street, he connected with the city water supply and, lo, his cans were again filled to the brim! Then he served street number two and again backed up to the fount to replenish his cans as before.

He proceeded in this way to serve each street, filling his cans with water after each street had been delivered, until all of his happy customers were served.

If forty quarts and one pint of pure milk remained in the cans after all his customers were attended to, how much pure milk must have been delivered on each of the four streets?

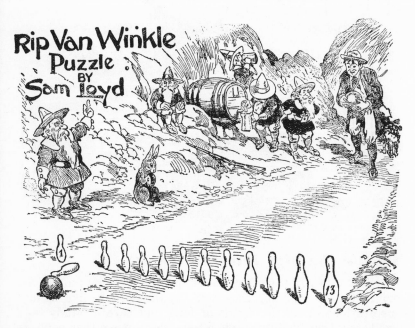

Rip Van Winkle Puzzle
BY Sam Loyd

6 How can Rip Van Winkle win the game?

THE OLD Dutch game of *Kugelspiel,* from which modern bowling is derived, used to be played with thirteen pins placed in a row. Only one or two pins could be knocked down by any single shot. The bowlers stood so close to the pins that it did not call for much skill to hit any single pin desired, or any two adjacent ones. Players bowled alternately, one ball at a time, and the point of the game was to see who could knock down the last pin.

The little Man-of-the-Mountain, with whom Rip Van Winkle is playing this game, has just rolled a ball and knocked out pin No. 2. Rip has a choice of twenty-two different plays: any one of the twelve single pins, or any one of the ten open spots that will bring down two adjacent pins. What is Rip's best shot to win the game? It is assumed that both players can hit any pin or pair of pins they wish, and that there is the best possible play on both sides.

7 *Divide the pigs into four pens.*

REPLYING TO the oft-repeated query as to how puzzles are originated — whether they come spontaneously like sudden inspirations or as the result of long and careful study — I would say that like other inventions they come either way. In both cases, the basic idea is usually suggested by some chance incident.

By way of illustration, let me tell this story. During a summer's bicycle outing I met a good-natured Hibernian whose apple orchard and spring of cool water made his little shanty a veritable "Mecca" for weary bicycle pilgrims. He was a unique character, with an inexhaustible stock of clever replies at his tongue's end, so that few of us ever bested him in a contest of wits.

When I mentioned that there was a certain bond of fellowship between us because we both made our living by the pen, he asked in his earnest way if I knew why an Irishman always builds a pig pen under the drawing-room window. After I had suggested all the explanations I could think of, he told me in a confidential whisper that could be heard a mile: "It was built there to keep the pigs in." He begged me not to tell the reason to the rest of my party, who might think it a joke. During our journey home there was not one of that party who did not fall off his bicycle while thinking over Pat's problem.

Of course, I thought about Pat's problem as well, and this led me to devise the following "odd" problem. Suppose that Pat has just twenty-one pigs. He keeps them in a rectangular pen and wishes to divide the pen by interior fences so that the pigs are divided into four pens, each pen containing an even number of pairs plus one odd pig. Can you show how this can be done?

8 *The Pig in the Garden.*

THE GATE was left open, and a pig entered the garden at the black square marked with the arrow. The pig visited every square of the garden, making only right-angle turns, then escaped by way of the white square at the open gate. Altogether, the pig made twenty right-angle turns.

The puzzle is to find the path with the least possible number of turns. The pig must enter and leave by the same squares, visit every square, make only right-angle turns, and must not cross the black bar in the upper left corner of the garden.

9 *The Five Newsboys*

FIVE CLEVER newsboys formed a partnership and disposed of their papers in the following manner. Tom Smith sold one paper more than one quarter of the whole lot, Billy Jones disposed of one paper more than a quarter of the remainder, Ned Smith sold one paper more than a quarter of what was left, and Charley Jones disposed of one paper more than a quarter of the remainder. At this stage, the Smith boys had together sold just one hundred papers more than the Jones boys had sold. Little Jimmy Jones, the youngest kid in the bunch, now sold all the papers that were left.

The three Jones boys sold more papers than the two Smith boys, but how many more?

10 *How old is Mary?*

AS A COMPANION piece to my famous problem of "How old is Ann?," and by way of apology to sister Mary who was slighted in the public controversy about her sister's age, we present the following problem:

"You see," remarked Grandpop, "the combined ages of Mary and Ann are forty-four years, and Mary is twice as old as Ann was when Mary was half as old as Ann will be when Ann is three times as old as Mary was when Mary was three times as old as Ann."

How old is Mary?

11 *Weary Willie*

WEARY WILLIE, a hobo who had outstayed his welcome at Joytown, started for Pleasantville simultaneously with the departure of Dusty Rhodes from Pleasantville. They met and exchanged the fraternal grip at a point where Willie had gone eighteen miles farther than Dusty. After an affectionate parting, it took Willie thirteen and one-half hours to reach Pleasantville, and Dusty twenty-four hours to get to Joytown. Assuming that each hobo traveled at a constant rate, how far was it from Pleasantville to Joytown?

THE MOON PROBLEM BY SAM LOYD

12 How long is the wire?

THERE IS a certain irresistible fascination about investigating affairs of the moon. When the famous "moon hoax" was sprung upon the public during the early part of the last century, it was shown that people were prepared to believe almost anything about the moon. The hoax was based on the alleged powers of a marvelous telescope, and the public seized upon the reports with such credulity that the hoaxers gave vivid descriptions of the inhabitants of the moon and their wonderful surroundings. Despite the extravagance of these descriptions, they were accepted as fact by many thousands of people.

Speculations about the state of affairs on the moon have come from many writers. Ariosto, in his *Orlando Furioso,* sent Astolpho on a venturesome trip to the moon, and his account of what he saw in the Valley of Lost Things deceived many. Cyrano de Bergerac's voyage to the moon is one of the most amusing contributions to literature, and Jules Verne's more recent story of a trip to the moon is perhaps the most thrilling of all lunar tales.

It was a detailed account by Edgar Allan Poe that so worked on the brain of a learned professor named Spearwood that he fitted out an expedition and actually undertook to make the trip by balloon. My sketch is drawn from a description published at the time of his ascent. The balloon is attached to a ball of wire, the wire being one hundredth of an inch thick. Assuming that the ball of wire was originally two feet in diameter, and further assuming that the wire was wound so solidly that there was no air space in the ball, can any of our puzzlists tell us the total length of the wire?

In my answer I will explain how the problem can be solved without having to be concerned with the value of *pi*.

13 *The Assassin's Bullet*

THE PICTURE above shows the face of a clock that was struck by the bullet from an assassin's pistol. The bullet struck the exact center of the face, driving the post through the works and stopping the clock. The two hands became united, as it were, on a single straight line, pointing in opposite directions, though not in the position shown. It is evident that the locked hands have rotated because they could not point directly at three and nine simultaneously.

Can you tell exactly what time it was when the bullet struck the clock?

THE FERRY BOAT PROBLEM
BY SAM LOYD

14 How wide is the river?

TWO FERRY boats start moving at the same instant from opposite sides of the Hudson River, one boat going from New York to Jersey City and the other going from Jersey City to New York. One boat is faster than the other, so they meet at a point 720 yards from the nearest shore.

After arriving at their destinations, each boat remains ten minutes in the slip to change passengers; then it starts on its return trip. The boats again meet at a point 400 yards from the other shore. What is the exact width of the river?

The problem shows how the average person, who follows the cut-and-dried rules of mathematics, will be puzzled by a simple problem that requires only a slight knowledge of elementary arithmetic. It can be explained to a child, yet I hazard the opinion that ninety-nine out of every hundred of our shrewdest businessmen would fail to solve it in a week. So much for learning mathematics by rule instead of common sense which teaches the reason why!

15 *Arrange nine matches to make ten, and six to make nothing.*

HARRY HAS given his sister nine matches that he challenges her to arrange so that they will look like ten. She in turn has given him six matches that he is to make look like nothing at all. These two simple tricks are not mathematical, but they will amuse the young folks who may not be familiar with the principle involved.

16 *Jack Sprat*

ACCORDING TO Mother Goose, Jack Sprat could eat no fat and his wife could eat no lean.

Together they could eat a barrel of fat pork in sixty days, whereas it would take Jack thirty weeks to perform this feat alone.

Together they could consume a barrel of lean pork in eight weeks, although his wife alone could not dispose of it in less than forty weeks.

Assuming that Jack would always eat lean pork whenever it was available and that his wife would do the same with fat, how long would it take both of them to eat a barrel of mixed pork, half fat and half lean?

THE MISER'S PUZZLE

17 How much gold did the miser have?

A CERTAIN miser, before he starved to death, hoarded up a quantity of five-, ten-, and twenty-dollar gold pieces. He kept them in five bags that were exactly alike in that each bag contained the same number of five-dollar pieces, the same number of ten-dollar pieces, and the same number of twenty-dollar pieces.

The miser counted his treasure by pouring it all on the table, then dividing it into four piles that were also exactly alike in containing the same amounts of each type of coin. His final step was to take any two of these piles, put them together, then divide their coins into three piles which were exactly alike in the sense already explained. It should now be an easy matter to guess the least amount of money that this poor old man could have had.

CROSS AND CRESCENT.

18 *Cut the crescent to make a cross.*

ASTONISHISHING AS it may seem, it is possible to cut the crescent moon shown above into as few as six pieces that can be fitted together to make a perfect Greek cross. The shape of the cross is shown in miniature on the head of the goddess. In forming the cross, it is necessary that one piece be turned over. [Note the straight line at each corner of the crescent and the fact that the two arcs of the crescent are arcs of the same size circle. — M.G.]

THE SCHOLAR'S PUZZLE

19 *Move one circle to make four rows.*

JENNIE, THE brightest little girl in school, is showing a clever puzzle to her classmate, Joe. After drawing six small circles on the fence, she said: "Now you can see only two rows with three circles in a line. I want you to mark out one circle and draw it somewhere else on the fence so that there will be four rows of three-in-a-line."

20 *Contracting Costs*

A CONTRACTOR planning the construction of a house found that he would have to pay:

$1,100 to the paper hanger and the painter,
$1,700 to the painter and plumber,
$1,100 to the plumber and electrician,
$3,300 to the electrician and carpenter,
$5,300 to the carpenter and mason,
$2,500 to the mason and paper hanger.

What does each man charge for his services?

A QUESTION OF TIME BY SAM LOYD.

21 *What time does the sign show?*

MOST CLOCK signs that hang in front of jewelry stores show the time to be almost twenty minutes after eight, as illustrated in the picture. Assuming that the two hands are the same distance from the six hour mark, exactly what time is indicated?

22 *Jack and Jill*

HERE IS a pretty puzzle from Mother Goose. Jack and Jill raced up and down a hill that was 440 yards from bottom to top. Jack got to the top first, immediately started down, and met Jill 20 yards from the top. He beat Jill to the bottom of the hill by half a minute. The record of the race is complicated by the fact that both runners were able to run downhill one-half again faster than they ran up. The puzzle is to figure out how long it took Jack to run the full half mile of 880 yards.

MILKMAN'S PUZZLE

3 *Measure two quarts for each lady.*

HONEST JOHN says: "What I don't know about milk is scarcely worth mentioning," but he was flabbergasted one day when each of two ladies asked him for two quarts of milk. One lady had a five-quart pail and the other had a four-quart pail. John had only two ten-gallon cans, each full of milk. How did he measure out exactly two quarts of milk for each lady?

It is a juggling trick pure and simple, devoid of trick or device, but it calls for much cleverness to get two quarts of milk into those two pails without making use of any receptacles other than the two pails and the two full cans.

24 *How can the trains pass?*

THIS IS a practical problem for railroad men, based on reminiscences of the days when railroading was in its infancy, before the introduction of double tracks, turn tables, and automatic switches. The good lady who furnished me with the subject matter of this puzzle based it upon a personal experience of what she called "the other day."

To tell the story in her own words, she said: "We had just arrived at the switch station, where the trains always pass, when we found that the Limited Express had broken down. I think the conductor man said that the smokestack had got hot and collapsed, so there was no draught to keep the engine operating."

The picture shows the Limited Express, with its collapsed smokestack, and the approach of the other train from Wayback, which, by some means or other, must pass the stalled train.

The sections on the switch marked A, B, C, and D are just large enough to accommodate one car or engine. Of course the broken-down engine cannot move on its own power, but must be pushed or pulled along as if it were a car. The cars may be drawn singly or coupled together in any required number, and the engine can pull with its front end as well as its back end.

The problem is to get the train from Wayback past the stalled train in the most efficient way possible, leaving the stalled train and its cars on the straight track, the cars and engine linked together in the same order as before and headed the same direction. By "most efficient possible way" we mean a way that requires the fewest number of direction reversals for the engine from Wayback.

To work on the puzzle, draw the tracks on a sheet of paper, then cut small counters of cardboard to represent the cars and engines.

5 *The Missing Link*

A FARMER had six pieces of chain of five links each, which he wanted made into an endless piece of thirty links.

If it costs eight cents to cut a link open and eighteen cents to weld it again, and if a new endless chain could be bought for a dollar and a half, how much would be saved by the cheapest plan.

26 *Cut the cake in two parts to make a square.*

THE SALESLADY is showing the children a piece of ginger-bread marked off in small squares that sell for a penny each. By cutting only along the lines, can you divide the gingerbread into two pieces that can be fitted together to make an eight-by-eight square?

[Loyd gives a second problem, but owing to the incomplete-ness of the text, it is not clear just what the problem is. No answer is given in the back of the *Cyclopedia*, so there is no way to reconstruct the question from the solution. My guess is that Loyd is asking his readers to divide the gingerbread along the lines into the two largest possible pieces that are the same size and shape. In any case, it is an interesting problem. We may assume that two pieces are the same shape if one can be turned over and superposed on the other. — M.G.]

27 *Texas Drovers*

THREE TEXAS drovers met on the highway and proceeded to dicker as follows.

Says Hank to Jim: "I'll give you six pigs for a hoss; then you'll have twice as many critters in your drove as I will have in mine."

Says Duke to Hank: "I'll give you fourteen sheep for a hoss; then you'll have three times as many critters as I."

Says Jim to Duke: "I'll give you four cows for a hoss; then you'll have six times as many critters as I."

From these interesting facts can you tell just how many animals were in each of the three droves?

28 *Tom the Piper's Son*

ACCORDING TO Mother Goose, Tom the Piper's son stole the pig and away he run. When Tom started after the pig, he was standing 250 yards due south of the pig. Both began running at the same time and ran with uniform speeds. The pig ran due east. Instead of running northeast on a straight line, Tom ran so that at every instant he was running directly toward the pig.

Assuming that Tom ran 1 and $\frac{1}{3}$ times faster than the pig, how far did the pig run before he was caught? The simple rule for solving this type of problem is based on elementary arithmetic, but will doubtless be new to most of our puzzlists.

29 *How old is Biddy?*

BIDDY WAS very sensitive on the matter of her age. For the last two score years she has invariably answered questions pertaining to her earthly sojourn by reciting the following little verse:

> *Five times seven and seven times three*
> *Add to my age and it will be*
> *As far above six nines and four*
> *As twice my years exceeds a score.*

This verse was doubtless quite correct when Biddy first recited it, but can you tell Biddy's present age?

30 *What numbers do the letters stand for?*

THE OWNER of a general store, who is something of a puzzlist, has put up this sign to see if any of his mathematical friends can translate it properly. Each different letter stands for a different digit. The words above the horizontal line represent numbers that add to the total of "ALL WOOL." The problem is to change all the letters to the correct digits.

It should be added that the owner of the store based his code on two key words of five letters each. He simply wrote one word after the other, then numbered their letters from 1 to 9, followed by zero.

31 *How Many Chickens?*

"NOW, MARIAH," said Farmer Jones to his wife, "if we should sell off seventy-five chickens, as I propose, our stock of feed would last just twenty days longer, whereas if we should buy a hundred extra chickens, as you suggest, we would run out of chicken feed fifteen days sooner."

"Well, now, Josiah," she replied, "how many chickens have we, anyhow?"

That's the problem. How many chickens did they have?

THE
LEANING
TOWER
~OF~
PISA
A classical
puzzle
BY
SAM LOYD.

32 *How far does the ball travel?*

IF AN elastic ball is dropped from the Leaning Tower of
Pisa at a height of 179 feet from the ground, and on each re-
bound the ball rises exactly one tenth of its previous height,
what distance will it travel before it comes to rest?

THE PATROLMAN'S PUZZLE

33 *Find a better route for Clancy.*

HERE IS a problem that has been puzzling Clancy ever since he got on the force. He patrols the forty-nine houses shown on his map, beginning and ending his tour at the spot he is pointing to with the end of his stick. His orders are to pass an uneven number of houses along any street or avenue before he makes a turn, and he cannot walk twice along any portion of his route.

The dotted line shows the route he has been following. It takes him past the twenty-eight houses that are shown white on the map. Can you help Clancy find a route that will comply with his orders and take him past the greatest possible number of houses? As before, the path must begin and end at the spot indicated by the policeman's stick.

34 *Three Problems concerning the Greek Cross*

THERE ARE many interesting cutting problems that involve the Greek cross shown on the giant Easter egg in the sketch. Here are three of them:

(1) Cut the cross into four pieces that will fit together to make a perfect square.

(2) Cut the cross into three pieces that will make a rhomboid.

(3) Cut the cross into three pieces that will make a rectangle twice as wide as it is high.

35 *Peddler Pete*

PEDDLER PETE got his accounts all tangled up because of the peculiar purchases of an eccentric old lady. First she bought some shoestrings. Then she bought four times as many packages of pins and finally she bought eight times as many handkerchiefs as shoestrings. Altogether she spent $3.24, paying for each article just as many cents as the number of that article that she bought. Peter wants to know just how many handkerchiefs the old lady bought.

36 *Transpose the flask and brush.*

THE SKETCH shows a migratory couple who have just moved into a cosy little six-room flat. They have five large pieces of furniture: bed, table, sofa, icebox, and bureau. The pieces are so bulky that no two can be placed at one time in any one room. It happened, however, that the furniture wreckers placed the icebox and bed in the wrong rooms. The man and his good wife have been trying for several hours to figure out an efficient plan for transposing them.

Being a systematic sort of fellow, the man marked out a diagram of his flat on the table, then placed five small articles on the squares to represent the pieces of furniture that are to be shifted. The whisky flask represents the bed, and the scrubbing brush is the icebox. You are asked to transpose these two pieces by moving one piece at a time into a vacant room.

Of course, there are a thousand and one ways of performing this simple trick, but keeping in mind Benjamin Franklin's well-known axiom that "three moves are as bad as a fire," the feat must be performed in the fewest possible number of moves.

37 *What is the track's circumference?*

HERE IS one of those curious and instructive problems that one is apt to pick up at any time during a morning's walk. Recently, while enjoying a walk in the country with a friend, we met his son on a cart drawn by a pony. The cart went around a sharp turn at a gait that threatened to upset the pony cart as well as the father's nerves. After we returned home, the father and son got into a lively discussion regarding the turning qualities of that pony cart.

In the picture, you see the son demonstrating his ability to drive the cart in a circle without upsetting it. The wheels of the cart are at the statutory distance of five feet apart on the axletree, and the outer wheels are making two turns to every single turn made by the inner ones. The problem is to guess the circumference of the circle described by the outer wheels.

38 *How old is Pocahontas?*

FARMER SMITH and his wife have fifteen children born at intervals of one year and a half. Pocahontas, the oldest child, admits that she is eight times as old as Captain John, Jr., the youngest of the brood.

How old is Miss Pocahontas?

39 *Which barrel was left?*

EACH BARREL in the above sketch contains either oil or vinegar. The oil sells for twice as much per gallon as the vinegar. A customer buys $14 worth of each, leaving one barrel. Which barrel did he leave?

40 *The Hat that didn't Sell*

UNABLE TO sell a hat for $20, a haberdasher lowered the price to $8. It still did not sell, so he cut the price again to $3.20, and finally to $1.28. One more mark-down and he will be selling the hat at cost. Assuming that he followed a system in making his price cuts, can you tell us what the next mark-down will be?

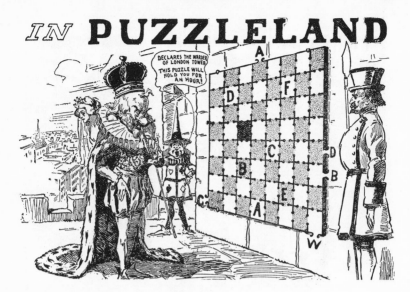

41 *Find the best routes.*

TOMMY RIDDLES is showing King Puzzlepate the famous problem of London Tower. Five guards are represented on the plan of the tower by the letters A, B, C, D, E. Promptly at the firing of a gun, which denotes the setting of the sun, guard A marches out by exit A, B exits at B, C exits at C, D exits at D, while E marches from his present cell to cell F. The problem is to discover how the five guards can make these five marches without any one man crossing the line of march of another. In other words, no more than one line of march is permitted through any one cell. Each man moves from cell to cell through the doors indicated on the plan. Tommy says it is a very simple trick when you know how.

Tommy has a second puzzle even better than the one just explained. Every night at midnight the warder enters the portal marked W and with stately tread marches through every one of the sixty-four rooms, ending at the black chamber where the young princes of Edward IV were supposed to have been murdered. By long practice the warder has discovered how to make this march without going through any room twice, and by making the fewest possible number of turns. Can any of our puzzlists find this route?

42 *Count out the boys.*

ALL PUZZLISTS are familiar with the ancient story of the
fifteen Christians and fifteen Turks who were caught at sea
in a storm, and how the captain decided that half of his passengers would have to be thrown overboard to save the ship.
Being a fair-minded man who believed that all should be
treated impartially, he arranged the thirty passengers in a
circle, then counted off every thirteenth man until fifteen un-
fortunate mortals had been selected. As the story goes, one of
the Christians was a mathematician and a devout man who
believed that Divine Providence had sent him to save the faith-
ful and destroy the unbelievers. Therefore, he arranged the
thirty passengers in such manner that every thirteenth man,
as the counting out proceeded, invariably proved to be a Turk.

This famous puzzle can be presented with playing cards,
using fifteen red cards and fifteen black. The problem is to
arrange the cards in a circle so that by counting round and
round, taking away every thirteenth card, only the blacks will
be removed. To solve the puzzle, simply place thirty cards in
a circle and count out every thirteenth card until fifteen have
been removed. Replace the remaining cards with red cards;

then fill the empty spaces with black cards, and the puzzle is solved!

This is all by way of introduction to the story illustrated in the above sketch. It chanced one day that ten children — five boys and five girls — returning from school, found five pennies. A little girl found the money, but Tommy Muttonhead claimed that since they were all together the "find" really belonged to the crowd. He was familiar with the Christians and Turks puzzle, so he thought it would be a great scheme to arrange everybody in a circle, then give a penny to the first five children who were counted out. The picture shows how Tommy arranged the girls. Beginning with the upper girl without a hat and counting clockwise, every thirteenth child will be a girl. Of course, as each child is counted out he is supposed to step back from the circle so he will not be included in the next counting. Tommy's scheme was to get the five pennies for the five boys, but he forgot that the plan was to give a penny to each child counted out, so it turned out that the girls got all the pennies and Tom got a good licking from the boys.

The problem is to guess the smallest number which Tommy should have used in place of thirteen in order to count out five boys instead of girls. You must also find the proper starting point for the counting.

43 *Cut the goose into three pieces that will fit together to form an egg of the size and shape shown.*

44 Coming to Town

UNCLE REUBEN and Aunt Cynthia came to town to shop. Reuben bought a suit and hat for $15. Cynthia paid as much for her hat as Reuben did for his suit; then she spent the rest of their money for a new dress.

On the way home, Cynthia called Reuben's attention to the fact that his hat cost $1 more than her dress. Then she added: "If we had divided our hat money differently so that we bought different hats, mine costing 1 and ½ times the cost of yours, then we each would have spent the same amount of money."

"In that case," said Uncle Reuben, "how much would my hat have cost?"

Can you answer Reuben's question and also tell how much money the couple spent altogether?

45 Bo-Peep's Pen

ACCORDING TO authorities on Mother Goose, the carpenter who constructed the sheepfold for Miss Bo-Peep discovered that he could save two posts by making the field square instead of oblong.

"Either way would hold the same number of sheep," he said, "but the square thing is to have a post for each sheep to tie to!"

How many sheep must there have been in this famous flock? Assume that the posts in both formations were set the same distance apart, that the areas of the square and oblong fields were the same, and that the flock consisted of less than three dozen sheep.

46 How old is Fido?

CHARLEY SLOWPOP was about to pop the matrimonial question to his girl friend when her little brother and his dog entered the living room.

"You can't tell a dog's age by the rings in his back," said *l'infant terrible,* "but five years ago my sister was five times as old as Fido, and now she is only three times as old!"

Charley Slowpop is very anxious to know Fido's age. Can you help him?

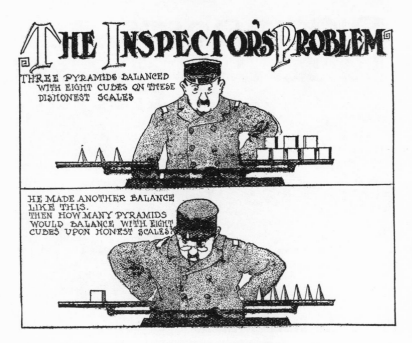

THE INSPECTOR'S PROBLEM

THREE PYRAMIDS BALANCED
WITH EIGHT CUBES ON THESE
DISHONEST SCALES

HE MADE ANOTHER BALANCE
LIKE THIS.
THEN HOW MANY PYRAMIDS
WOULD BALANCE WITH EIGHT
CUBES UPON HONEST SCALES?

47 *How much does a cube weigh?*

INSPECTOR JONES, whose duty it is to check on the accuracy of various balance scales in use throughout the town, has just discovered a pair of dishonest scales. One arm is longer than the other, but the pans are so weighted as to balance. (You must not judge from appearances in the sketch, for with a puzzle-maker's license I have drawn the scales so as to give no clue to the puzzle.)

When the inspector put three pyramid weights on the long arm, they balanced with eight cube weights on the short arm. But when he put one cube on the long arm, it balanced six pyramids on the other! Assuming that the true weight of a pyramid is one ounce, can you guess the true weight of a cube?

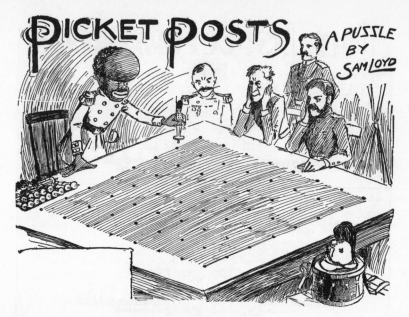

48 *Place the sixteen men.*

HERE IS an odd little problem in military tactics that can be worked out advantageously on an ordinary checkerboard of sixty-four squares. The puzzle is to place sixteen checkers on the board so that there will not be more than two in a row vertically, horizontally, or diagonally. There is one stipulation. The first two men must be placed on two of the four central squares of the board.

If all sixteen men are posted correctly, a cannon ball coming from any possible direction could not hit more than two men. It is a pretty and interesting puzzle, somewhat akin to the famous problem of placing eight queens on a chessboard so that no queen can be taken by another.

49 *Against the Wind*

A BICYCLE rider rode a mile in three minutes with the wind, and returned in four minutes against the wind. Assuming that at all times he applies the same force to his pedals, how long would it take him to ride a mile if there were no wind?

MERRY GO ROUND PUZZLE

50 *How many children are on the carousel?*

WHILE ENJOYING a giddy ride on the carousel, Sammy propounded this problem: "One third of the number of kids riding ahead of me, added to three quarters of those riding behind me gives the correct number of children on this merry-go-round."

How many children were riding the carousel?

51 *Change the Turkish emblem to the Crusader's cross.*

THE PICTURE shows an incident during one of the great battles of the Crusades. It is related that after a body of Christian knights captured a Turkish fort, "they threw the Saracen soldiers from the battlements and in full view of the opposing armies changed the banners on the walls."

The story seems to imply that there is a simple way of converting the Turkish flag into the emblem of the crusaders. Assume that the Turkish flag shown above consists of a dark piece of cloth with holes cut in the shapes of a star and a crescent and mounted on a white cloth to make a white emblem. The problem is this. Cut the dark cloth into the fewest number of pieces that can then be shifted in position to make a white emblem of a cross like the one shown on the knight's shield.

52 *Mrs. Wiggs' Cabbages*

MRS. WIGGS explained to Lovey Mary that she has a larger square cabbage patch now than she had last year, and will therefore raise 211 more cabbages. How many of our mathematicians and agriculturists can guess the number of cabbages Mrs. Wiggs will raise this year?

53 *Arrange the digits and dots so they add to 100.*

When the centennial of 1776 was celebrated in Philadelphia, I designed a little arithmetical puzzle that gave rise to considerable discussion. The problem was to arrange the ten digits and the four dots in such a way that they formed numbers that would add up to exactly 100. [No other mathematical symbols are to be used, but it should be noted that the dots may be used either as decimals or above a digit to indicate that it is a repeating decimal. (For example, .i̇ tells us that the decimal expands to an endless series of 1's. It is equal, of course, to exactly 1/9.) — M.G.]

A·DAISY·
PUZZLE·GAME
BY SAM LOYD.

57 *How can the second player always win?*

IN THE SUMMER of 1865, when I was with a party of tourists who were tramping over the snows of Switzerland from Altdorf to Fluelen, we met a little peasant girl gathering daisies. Thinking to amuse the child, I showed her how to learn her matrimonial future by plucking off the petals of a flower to find out if she would be the bride of the "rich man, poor man, beggar man, or thief." She said that the sport was well known to the country lassies, with this difference: two people played the game, each at liberty to pluck a single petal or two adjacent ones. The game continued by singles or doubles until the victor took the last petal, leaving the stem called the "old maid" with the loser of the game.

To our intense astonishment little Gretchen, who could not have been more than ten, vanquished our entire party by winning every game, no matter who played first. I did not study out the trick until we were back in Lucerne, but I was so bantered by the party that I made quite a point of investigating the game.

I will say, incidentally, that I returned to Altdorf some years later and visited the locality of my previous defeat. It would give me pleasure if I could add to the romance of the story by saying that I found little Gretchen developed into a beautiful *fraulein,* with a phenomenal mathematical bent. I doubtless saw her, however, for the entire female population of the *dorf* were preparing to sow the fall crops. They were all prematurely old and exactly alike, and I imagined I recognized my former friend harnessed up with a cow to a plow, which was guided through the soil by her noble husband.

The game is shown above in the form of a daisy with thirteen petals. It can be played by two persons who take turns placing small markers on the petals. At each play one may cover one petal or two adjacent ones. The person who covers the last petal wins, leaving the "old maid" stump to his opponent.

Can any of our puzzlists tell us who should win this game, the first or second player, and what system he should follow in order to win?

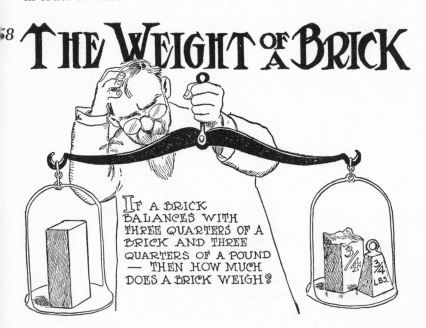

58

THE WEIGHT OF A BRICK

IF A BRICK BALANCES WITH THREE QUARTERS OF A BRICK AND THREE QUARTERS OF A POUND — THEN HOW MUCH DOES A BRICK WEIGH?

59 *Move four ships to make five rows with four ships in each.*

TEN BATTLESHIPS are shown here in two rows. When the enemy approaches, four ships change their positions to make five rows with four ships in each row. How is this done? Ten coins may be used for working on the puzzle.

50 Cut the two pieces to make one circle.

ALMOST EVERY collection of puzzles contains a certain problem about a joiner who wished to convert a circular table top into two oval stool tops with hand holes in the center as shown above. The puzzle was to do it in the fewest number of pieces.

The solution to be found in the puzzle books required eight pieces. The circle is cut as shown in Figure 1; then two stool tops are formed as shown in Figure 2.

According to our recently discovered method, which introduces the Chinese Monad symbol, the problem can be solved by cutting the circular top into as few as six pieces. The problem is presented here in reversed form. Cut each oval piece into three parts so that the six pieces will form a circular table top without holes.

61 How many ways can you read "Red Rum and Murder"?

IN FORMER days, when word puzzles were in vogue, much brain work was given to the construction of words and sentences that would read the same backward as well as forward. They were known as palindromes. There are many words, such as "level," "eve," "gig," which read the same either way, but the aim was rather to construct palindromic sentences such as Adam's noted greeting to Eve, "Madam, I'm Adam," or the sentence, "Name no one man." The palindrome is of very ancient origin, and there are some classical specimens in Latin and French that are often quoted.

Shown above is an old palindromic puzzle that I perpetrated in my early days for the benefit of a temperance organization, and which will try the patience and skill of our young puzzlists. The problem is to determine just how many different ways one can read the warning, "Red Rum & Murder," without being affected by delirium tremens. Commence at any of the "R's," including those inside the square, and spell the phrase by moving up or down, left or right, or diagonally to an adjacent letter.

THE MONAD PUZZLE

52 *How should the Monad be divided?*

THE MONAD, the great religious symbol of China, was adopted in this country by the Northern Pacific Railway Company as its official trade-mark. It can be seen on the company's freight cars, bonds, stock certificates, advertisements, and time tables. In 1893 at the Chicago World's Fair, Chief Engineer Henry McHenry saw the Monad on a Korean flag and persuaded the Northern Pacific to adopt it as an emblem. The most interesting thing I ever heard about the sign was told to me by P. H. Tighe, the famous manufacturer of baseballs, who said that he got the idea of the two-piece cover from the shape of the Monad.

Several books have been written about the symbol and the various interpretations that oriental scholars have put upon it. As a rule these explanations are so mixed up with oriental theology about the male and female forces of nature and the "illimitable as adverse to the great extreme" that the reader feels as if he were reading about the Keely motor.

One writer on the subject is of the opinion that the sign has some recondite mathematical significance, and quotes ancient Chinese works as saying: "The illimitable produces the great extreme. The great extreme produces the two principles. The two principles produce the four quarters, and from the four quarters we develop the quadrature of the eight diagrams of Feuh-hi." This was written more than three thousand years ago and is suggestive of the following three puzzles.

1. This is given as a simple puzzle for young folks. With one continuous line, divide the black and white parts of the Monad (known respectively as the Yin and Yang) so that the circle will be divided into four pieces of the same size and shape.

2. With one straight line, divide the Yin and Yang so that each is cut into two pieces of equal area.

3. Cut each of the two horseshoe shapes shown below (one dark and the other white) into two pieces in such a way that the four pieces can be put together to make the Monad.

63 *How far to Piketown?*

AN ENGLISH tourist in the wild and woolly West was informed at the hotel that there were four different ways he could travel to Piketown.

1. He could ride the stagecoach all the way. This included one stopover of thirty minutes at a certain wayhouse along the road.

2. He could walk all the way. If he started walking at the same time the coach left the hotel, the coach would beat him to Piketown by one mile.

3. He could walk to the wayhouse and then take the coach. If he and the coach left the hotel at the same time, the coach would arrive at the wayhouse at the time he had walked four miles. But because of the thirty-minute wait, he would arrive just as the coach was leaving so that he would be able to ride it on to Piketown.

4. He could take the coach to the wayhouse, then walk the rest of the way. This was the fastest procedure, getting him to Piketown fifteen minutes ahead of the coach.

How far is it from the hotel to Piketown?

PUZZLING SCALES

64 How many glasses will balance with the bottle?

65 *How much profit did the town make?*

HERE IS an elementary puzzle in bookkeeping that should give no trouble to anyone who understands the principles of profit and loss. I give it because it is based on an actual occurrence that was reported to me for a decision. Since all parties to the transaction held different views, it seemed to me it would furnish a capital theme for a puzzle.

A temperance town in New Hampshire appointed an agent for one year to be the only person authorized to sell liquors. They advanced him $12 cash and liquors that had a value of $59.50 wholesale. In rendering his accounts at the end of the year, the agent showed extra liquor purchases to the extent of $283.50. His total sales amounted to $285.80, on which he received a commission of five per cent in lieu of salary.

The sketch shows the agent and town committee taking account of their stock at the end of the year. Each item is marked with its retail price. The puzzle is to tell how much profit the town made on its liquor sales. This involves, of course, determining by what per cent the agent increased the wholesale value of his stock in order to realize a profit.

56 *The Three Beggars*

A CHARITABLE lady met a poor man to whom she gave one cent more than half of the money she had in her purse. The poor fellow, who was a member of the United Mendicants' Association, managed, while tendering his thanks, to chalk the organization's sign of "a good thing" on her clothing. As a result, she met many objects of charity as she proceeded on her journey.

To the second applicant she gave two cents more than half of what she had left. To the third beggar she gave three cents more than half of the remainder. She now had one penny left. How much money did she have when she started out?

57 *Puzzling Prattle*

TWO CHILDREN, who were all tangled up in their reckoning of the days of the week, paused on their way to school to straighten matters out.

"When the day after tomorrow is yesterday," said Priscilla, "then 'today' will be as far from Sunday as that day was which was 'today' when the day before yesterday was tomorrow!"

On which day of the week did this puzzling prattle occur?

58 *The Telegraph Poles*

ON AN automobile trip the other day I passed a line of telegraph poles that was 3 and 5/8 miles long. With the aid of a stop watch I discovered that the number of poles that passed per minute, multiplied by 3 and 5/8, equaled the number of miles per hour that I was traveling. Assuming that the poles were equally spaced and that I traveled at a constant speed, what was the distance between two adjacent poles?

59 *An Odd Catch*

ASK YOUR friends if they can write down five odd figures that will add up to fourteen. It is really astonishing how engrossed most people will get, and how much time they will spend over this seemingly simple problem. You must be careful, however, to say "figures" and not "numbers."

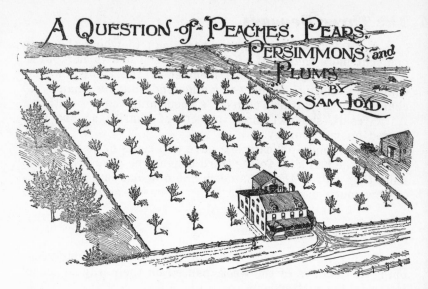

A QUESTION of PEACHES, PEARS, PERSIMMONS and PLUMS BY SAM LOYD.

70 *How are the four sets grouped?*

I ONCE knew an eccentric old gardener who made a practice of setting out his young fruit trees according to a secret code, so that no one but himself could locate the several varieties of trees in his orchard. He gave as his reason the fact that he was engaged in experimental grafting and did not care to let visitors, or even those in his employ, into the secrets of his craft.

The last time I saw him he had just set out sixty young trees in the field adjoining his house, as shown in the accompanying picture. These sixty trees were what is known as quince stock, upon which the different varieties of fruit are grafted. It had always been his practice to graft one variety of fruit on ten trees in such a way that the trees would form five straight rows with four in each row. He asked me if it would be possible to do this with four different varieties of fruit — peaches, pears, persimmons, and plums — and I found it to be quite a pretty little puzzle.

A good way to work on the puzzle is to draw an eight-by-eight checkerboard on a large sheet of paper. Eliminate the four cells at the bottom where the gardener's house stands. To represent the four varieties of fruit, use forty playing cards containing ten of each of the four suits. Now see if you can place the forty cards on the sixty cells of the checkerboard so that each suit will form five straight rows with four cards in each row. Of course, no more than one card can go on any one cell.

1 *Sawing the Checkerboard*

THIS CLEVER young carpenter received a chest of tools for a Christmas present, and immediately set to work to make a fine chessboard to present to Dr. Lasker, the chess champion of the world. Dr. Lasker is a great mathematician and puzzlist as well as a marvelous chess player, but can he beat our puzzlists in discovering the largest number of different pieces that the carpenter could have used in making this board?

Each piece must be made up of squares. One piece can be a single black square, another piece a single white square. Only one piece may consist of two squares, because all two-square pieces are alike. But a three-square piece has four different forms — a straight row with a black square in the middle, a straight row with a white square in the middle, a crooked piece with one black square, and a crooked piece with one white square. When you have divided the checkerboard into the greatest number of different pieces, you will have solved the puzzle.

The Tinker's Puzzle
— BY —
SAM LOYD

72 *How large is the top of the kettle?*

THE TINKER in the above sketch has just finished making a flat-bottomed kettle that is twelve inches deep and holds exactly twenty-five gallons of water. How many of our mathematicians can give us (to the nearest inch) the diameter of the kettle's brim, assuming that it is twice the diameter of the bottom?

73 *The Disappointed Pensioners*

A KIND lady who dispensed charity each week to some needy persons hinted to her pensioners that each would receive two dollars more if there were five applicants less. Each mendicant endeavored to persuade the others to keep away, but at the next meeting everyone was on hand including four new applicants. As a result, each man got one dollar less.

Assuming that the lady distributed the same amount of money each week, can you guess how much this amount was?

74 *Arrange the volumes to make nine different fractions.*

WHEN I was a boy, I was given nine ponderous volumes of Hume's *History of England*, accompanied by promises galore of guns, ponies, and everything else if I would only study those books. I must confess that what I don't know about the history of England would more than double the size of an ordinary library, but I did discover some interesting puzzles based on those weighty volumes.

I found, for example, that by placing the volumes on two shelves as shown in the sketch, the fraction 6729/13458 is exactly equal to 1/2. Is it possible to find other arrangements, using all nine volumes, that will make fractions equivalent to 1/3, 1/4, 1/5, 1/6, 1/7, 1/8, and 1/9?

75 *Spell the hidden couplet.*

TOMMY RIDDLES is calling the King's attention to a wonderfully educated spelling bee. You will observe that each of the cells on the beehive contains a letter. If the bee starts at the proper cell, then crawls from cell to adjacent cell, it can spell out the opening two lines of a familiar poem. Can you find the route that will spell the concealed couplet?

76 *Lord Rosslyn's System*

TWO LADS, each with the same amount of cash, played the races using Lord Rosslyn's system of placing as many dollars on the weakest horse as the track offers odds of so many dollars to a single dollar.

Jim backed Kohinoor to win, while Jack bet on him for second place, so they put up different amounts at different odds, although the amount of their bets together was equal to half of their combined capital. They both won, but when they cashed their winnings and counted the money, Jim had twice as much as Jack.

Now, remembering that bets must be made in full dollars (no fractions of dollars being permitted), can you guess the amounts that each boy won?

77 ***What are the people watching?***

YOUNG HARRY was such a cautious fellow that he was reluctant to pay for his admission to the circus until he knew how large the circus was. He is shown here asking the man at the gate to tell him the number of horses, riders, and animals owned by the circus.

The gatekeeper, somewhat ashamed of the meager display of wonders within the tent as compared to the glowing pictures on the posters outside, feigned ignorance of the exact number of marvelous attractions. He explained that in addition to the horses and riders, who possessed altogether 100 feet and 36 heads, there was a collection of African jungle animals which brought the sum total up to 56 heads and 156 feet.

We ask our readers to tell the number of horses and number of riders owned by the circus as well as the nature of the attraction in that cage to the left of the picture, which seems to be the most popular exhibit in the circus zoo.

78 *How much did the farmer get for his melons?*

IN PUZZLELAND all business transactions are made on the basis of interesting mathematical problems. For example, Farmer Jones disposed of his melons by selling his first customer exactly half of his supply plus half of a melon. The second purchaser took one third of what remained, plus one third of a melon. The next customer purchased a fourth of what remained, plus one fourth of a melon. Then he sold a fifth of what was left plus one fifth of a melon. All of these melons were sold for a dollar a dozen. He then disposed of all the melons he had left at a price of thirteen for a dollar. Assuming that the farmer started out with less than a thousand melons, can you tell how much money he received altogether for his stock?

The little boy on the right of the picture is forming a pyramid with musk melons. He wishes to make two triangular pyramids (that is, pyramids whose bases and sides are all equilateral triangles) of such size that he can then combine the melons in both pyramids and construct a larger triangular pyramid without having any melons left over. What size should his pyramids be?

[Loyd does not give an answer to his pyramid piling problem. In the picture, the farm boy is clearly building a square-based pyramid. If Loyd intended to ask for the sizes of two tetrahedral pyramids that can be combined to make one square-based pyramid, then the answer is easy. Any two tetrahedral pyramids with sides that are consecutive numbers will combine to make a square pyramid (for example, a tetrahedron formed with four melons will combine with one of ten melons — the sides are two and three, respectively — to give fourteen melons that will form a pyramid based on a square of nine melons).

If Loyd's problem is correctly stated, the simplest answer is that two piles of ten melons each will make one pile of twenty melons. If Loyd intended the two smaller piles to be of different sizes, what is the simplest answer?—M.G.]

79 *Squaring the Swastika*

Cut the swastika into four pieces that will form a square.

THE REMNANT ~ ~ PUZZLE

BY SAM LOYD

80 Cut in three pieces to make a square.

THE LADY is displaying an odd-shaped piece of cloth that she wishes to cut into three pieces that will form a perfect square.

The triangular piece may also be placed in the two positions shown below, and the problem can still be solved by cutting into three pieces.

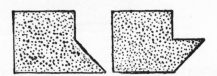

81 *How many squashes will the farmers lose?*

TWO HAYSEEDS, who know nothing about an acre of land containing 43,560 square feet, are discussing a deal they have just concluded with Farmer Sykes' boy, who is fresh out of college. They traded him their squash field, which they have drawn on the right door of the barn, for his squash field shown on the other barn door. The two farmers think they have outsmarted the Sykes boy because their old lot is surrounded by fewer rails than his.

As you can see, their old lot has 140 rails on one side and 150 on the other, making 580 rails in all. The field they have just acquired is 110 by 190 rails, or 600 rails altogether. Of course, Farmer Sykes' boy has learned enough elementary geometry to know that the closer a rectangle is to a square, the greater its area in proportion to its perimeter, so that in this case he actually got a field that is a bit larger than the field he traded for it.

Supposing that 840 squashes are raised per acre on both fields, can anyone tell us exactly how many squashes per acre on their old lot those farmers are going to lose?

Trading in the Philippines
a problem by
Sam Loyd.

82 *What are the weights of the four rings?*

I RECENTLY came upon an old travel book that described some of the primitive methods once used for conducting business in the Philippines. The traveling merchant shown in the picture uses a balance scale and four metal rings that serve as weights. The rings are of different weights and sizes, and he carries them on his arms like bracelets.

With these four rings, the trader can weigh anything from a quarter of a pound up to ten pounds. A similar trick in juggling weights on balance scales is given in many puzzle books, but it is not so clever as this one which enables the trader to get within a quarter of a pound of any weight within the limits mentioned.

What are the weights of the four rings?

83 *The Two Watches*

I STARTED two watches at the same time and found that one of them went two minutes per hour too slow and the other went one minute per hour too fast. When I looked at them again, the faster one was exactly one hour ahead of the other. How long had the watches been running?

84 *How many eggs can go in the crate?*

THE TWO hens are trying to figure out how many eggs they can put in that crate without having more than two eggs in any row, including all the diagonal rows. Two eggs have already been placed, so no more eggs are permitted on that corner-to-corner diagonal.

85 *Losing at Cinch*

I WAS initiated into the mysteries of the card game of cinch while traveling on the steamship "Bacteria." I lost the first game to Baron von D and Count de C, who each won enough to double their chips.

The baron and I scored the second game, thereby doubling our assets. Then the count and I won the third game, which doubled our chips. The mysterious feature of the situation was that each player won twice and lost only once, after which each player had the same number of chips.

I found that I had lost $100. How much money did I start with?

86 *How old is the boy?*

"WHAT IS the age of that boy?" asked the conductor. Flattered by this interest shown in his family affairs, the suburban resident replied:

"My son is five times as old as my daughter, and my wife is five times as old as the son, and I am twice as old as my wife, whereas grandmother, who is as old as all of us put together, is celebrating her eighty-first birthday today."

How old was the boy?

87 *Longfellow's Bees*

THE POET Longfellow, in his novel *Kavanagh,* introduced several clever mathematical problems from an ancient Sanskrit work. The following is one of them:

"If one fifth of a hive of bees flew to the ladamba flower, one third flew to the slandbara, three times the difference of these two numbers flew to an arbor, and one bee continued to fly about, attracted on each side by the fragrant ketaki and the malati, what was the number of bees?"

88 *Common Stock*

"GENTLEMEN," SAID Chauncy at a directors' meeting, "the present income from the earnings of the road would pay six per cent on the entire stock issue, but since there is $4,000,000 of preferred stock on which we pay seven and one half per cent interest, we are therefore able only to pay five per cent interest on the common stock."

What was the worth of the common stock?

89 *Dirty Linen*

CHARLIE AND Freddy took their soiled collars and cuffs, thirty pieces in all, to a Chinese laundry. When Freddy picked up his bundle a few days later, he found that it contained half the cuffs and one third of the collars, and cost him 27 cents. Four cuffs cost the same as five collars. How much will Charlie be charged for the rest of their laundry?

The Reaper's Problem
BY SAM LOYD.

90 *How wide should the strip be?*

MECHANICS AND laborers who have no great skills in mathematics will often solve, in a practical way, some very difficult problems. I call the attention of our puzzlists to the clever way in which a couple of farmers adjusted their affairs.

A Texas ranchman, who owned more land than he could conveniently farm, leased half of a certain field to a neighbor. This field was 2,000 yards long by 1,000 yards wide, but because of certain bad streaks which ran through the land it was decided that a fairer division would be obtained by cutting a band around the field than by dividing it in half.

I presume our puzzlists will find no great difficulty in determining the width of a border strip, to be cut all around that field, that will contain exactly half of the total crop. There is a simple rule which will apply to any rectangular field.

PUZZLE OF GRAND FATHER'S CLOCK BY SAM LOYD

91 *When did the clock stop?*

THERE IS a legend back of the familiar song about the grandfather's clock that was "too tall for the shelf, so it stood ninety years on the floor." It seems that the clock had the incurable habit of stopping whenever the minute hand attempted to pass the hour hand. Advancing age made the old gentleman more irritable, and once when the hands came together and stopped the clock, he flew into such an ungovernable passion that he fell down dead. It was then that:

> The clock stopped short,
> Never to go again,
> When the old man died.

A photograph of the stopped clock was shown to me, with its classical figure of a female figure representing time. It struck me as remarkable that with the knowledge that the hour and minute hands were together, it was possible to figure out the exact time from the position of the second hand alone, as shown above.

92 *Archery Puzzle*

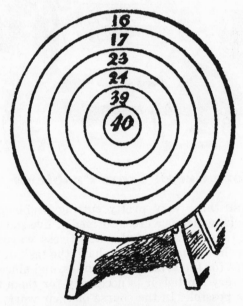

How many arrows does it take to score exactly 100 on this target?

93 *Three more Greek Cross Problems*

HERE ARE three very pretty cutting problems involving the Greek cross, which is a cross formed of five squares like the cross you see on the side of the Red Cross wagon. The Red Cross lassies shown in the picture have the task of cutting red flannel crosses for the arms of the nurses, and since the supply of flannel is very limited, it is necessary for them to waste as little cloth as possible. In the course of their work, the following problems arose:

(1) Cut a square into five pieces that will fit together without any waste to make two Greek crosses of the same size.

(2) Cut a square into five pieces that will fit together to make two Greek crosses of *different* size.

(3) Cut a Greek cross into five pieces that will form two smaller Greek crosses of the same size. This is one of the most beautiful of all cutting problems involving the Greek cross.

CROSS-COUNTRY-RUNNING PROBLEM BY SAM LOYD.

94 *How far apart are the bridges?*

ALTHOUGH THE boys are running in opposite directions, they are both racing to the same spot, marked by the American flag in the upper left corner of the scene. The boy on the right will make a right-angle turn to the left when he reaches the bridge; then he will cross the canal and continue on the road until he reaches the goal. The boy on the left will make an acute-angle turn when he reaches another bridge that is not visible in the picture. He will then cut across the field, through the drove of cows, in a straight line toward the flag.

The boy on the right has 250 yards to run before he makes his turn, then 600 more yards to go before he comes to the flag. If this same boy were to turn around and take the other route, he would find the distance to be exactly the same. This means that the boy on the left has a good head-start, so if he can run as fast as the other boy, he should win easily.

The problem is to determine the distance in yards between the two bridges. Assume that the boys are now running in opposite directions on the base of a right triangle, the ends of which are the two bridges. The boy on the left, after he reaches the bridge not shown, will then take the hypotenuse of the right triangle.

95 *How many apples and roses did each get?*

THE ANCIENT Greek fragment about how the Graces and the Muses divided their golden apples and their flowers has been ascribed to different ages and to as many different authors. The mathematical feature has been credited to Euclid and Archimedes, though it is known that Homer sang many centuries before of the daughters of Zeus with their roses and apples.

The story would be clearer to our puzzlists if I gave the original Greek, but he is away, and since our font of Greek type is somewhat out of sorts, I am compelled to give what might be called a very free translation, keeping as close as possible to the literal wording of the original. It differs materially from the meaningless version so often found in puzzle books.

> As through Olympian garden bowers
> Strolled three fair Graces, culling flowers
> Of perfume rare and varied hue,
> Of pink and white and red and blue,
> They chanced nine Muses fair to meet,
> With golden stores of applies sweet.
> Each Muse in turn, to every Grace
> Some applies gave, and in their place
> Such roses did receive as made
> Their stores all just alike, 'twas said.

> Now, if the numbers were the same,
> The quantities of each proclaim!

To make this clearer, let us say that there were nine Muses each with roses of four different colors — pink, white, red, blue — who met three Graces with golden apples. Each Muse gave some roses to each Grace; then each Grace gave some apples to each Muse.

After this exchange, each girl had the same number of apples, the same number of red roses, and the same number of white, pink, and blue roses. Moreover, the number of apples possessed by each girl was equal to the number of roses that she had.

What are the smallest quantities of apples and roses of each color that will fit these conditions?

6 *Dunce Puzzle*

How CAN these three little boys arrange themselves so that the digits marked on their clothes will form a three-digit number evenly divisible by seven?

97 *Cut the quilt to make two squares.*

THE MAN and wife in the above sketch are discussing ways and means of making two square patchwork quilts from the one quilt shown. Because of the checkered pattern, it can be cut only along the vertical and horizontal lines that form the squares. The problem is to cut the large quilt into the fewest number of pieces that will fit together again to make two squares.

98 *O'Shaugnessy's Estate*

IN THE exuberance of his joy at the prospect of becoming a happy father in his old age, O'Shaugnessy vowed to settle two thirds of his estate upon "the boy" and one third upon the mother, but in case "the boy" should be a girl, then two thirds of the estate should go to the mother and one third to the daughter. When it developed, however, that "the boy" was a twin, which made it necessary to provide for both a boy and a girl, as well as the mother, O'Shaugnessy's mind was not in a state to decide upon the proper way to carry out the terms of his promise.

What do our friends, especially members of the legal profession who have shown so much interest in these problems, say should be the proper division of O'Shaugnessy's estate?

DIVIDING HIS FLOCKS
BY SAM LOYD

How many sons did the rancher have?

A WESTERN rancher, finding himself well advanced in years, called his boys together and told them that he wished to divide his herds between them while he yet lived.

"Now, John," he said to the eldest, "you may take as many cows as you think you could conveniently care for, and your wife Nancy may have one ninth of all the cows left."

To the second son he said, "Sam, you may take the same number of cows that John took, plus one extra cow because John had the first pick. To your good wife, Sally, I will give one ninth of what will be left."

To the third son he made a similar statement. He was to take one cow more than the second son, and his wife was to have one ninth of those left. The same applied to the other sons. Each took one cow more than his next oldest brother, and each son's wife took one ninth of the remainder.

After the youngest son had taken his cows, there were none left for his wife. Then the rancher said: "Since horses are worth twice as much as cows, we will divide up my seven horses so that each family will own livestock of equal value."

The problem is to tell how many cows the rancher owned and how many sons he had.

THE MISSING NUMBER

100 Supply the missing digit.

THE CHINESE are wonderfully expert at figures. The professor in the illustration asked me to write down any two numbers, provided that in forming them I used only the nine digits and zero. For example, I could write:

342195
6087

Each digit was to be used once and once only. I was then told to add the two numbers. Finally, I was asked to erase the two numbers as well as any digit I pleased in the answer. The professor glanced at the answer and quickly told me the missing digit.

The slate in the picture shows my answer. Can you supply the missing digit and explain how the Chinese mathematician was able to guess it so quickly?

BEATING THE RECORD ~ BY SAM LOYD

1 How fast did the horse trot?

DURING A recent performance of the trotting queen, Lou Dillon, I was struck by an odd little problem that arose and that proved to be too much for the limited mathematical knowledge of the timekeepers. It appears that one timekeeper clocked only the first three quarters of a mile, and a second timekeeper recorded only the last three quarters. The horse ran the first three quarters in 81 and 3/8 seconds, and the last three quarters in 81 and 1/4 seconds. Assuming that the horse ran the first half of the mile in the same time that she ran the last half, how many of our puzzlists can tell us the time for the whole mile?

[Loyd gives a solution to this problem, but without additional data there is no unique answer. Perhaps some sentences were carelessly omitted when the problem was set in type for the *Cyclopedia*. In any case, to make Loyd's answer unique, assume that the times also are equal for the third and last quarter. — M.G.]

102   *Put the elephant in the center of the flag.*

TOMMY RIDDLES, the court page, announces that the King of Siam (who aspires to the hand of Princess Enigma) wishes to show King Puzzlepate a puzzle based on his country's flag. The problem is to cut the flag into the smallest number of pieces that can be refitted together so as to bring the white elephant into the middle of the flag.

In the second puzzle, Princess Enigma tests the cleverness of her royal suitor by showing a plan of her favorite orchard. It contains eight apple trees and eight pear trees, each tree being represented by a specimen of fruit. The puzzle is to begin at any one of the eight pears. Mark out the shortest possible route that will go through all sixteen pieces of fruit and end at the heart to which the Princess is pointing. The numbers are placed on the fruit merely to enable competitors to describe their answers clearly. See if you can find a shorter route than the one marked out by the King of Siam.

How large was the farm?

FARMER SYKES complained that he had agreed to pay $80 cash and a fixed number of bushels of wheat as the yearly rental of his farm. That, he explained, would amount to just $7 an acre when wheat was worth 75 cents a bushel. But now wheat was worth $1 a bushel, so he was paying $8 per acre, which he thought was too much.

How large was the farm?

Turkey vs. Goose

MRS. O'FLAHERTY purchased some turkeys at twenty-four cents a pound and the same weight of geese at eighteen cents a pound. Mrs. Smith tells her that she might have gained an additional two pounds if she had followed the rule given in *Hints to Boarding-house Keepers* which states: "For Christmas, divide your money evenly between turkey and goose."

What was the total amount of Mrs. O'Flaherty's purchase?

What did the suit sell for?

"JOHNNIE, MY BOY," said a successful merchant to his little son, "it is not what we pay for things but what we get for them that makes good business. I gained ten per cent on that fine suit of clothes I just sold, whereas if I had bought it ten per cent cheaper and sold it for twenty per cent profit, it would have sold for twenty-five cents less. Now, what did I get for that suit?"

How old is Jimmy?

"YOU SEE," said Mrs. Murphy, "Paddy is now one and one-third times as old as he was when he took to drink, and little Jimmy, who was forty months old when Paddy took to drink, is now two years more than half as old as I was when Paddy took to drink, so when little Jimmy is as old as Paddy was when he took to drink, our three ages combined will amount to just one hundred years."

How old is little Jimmy?

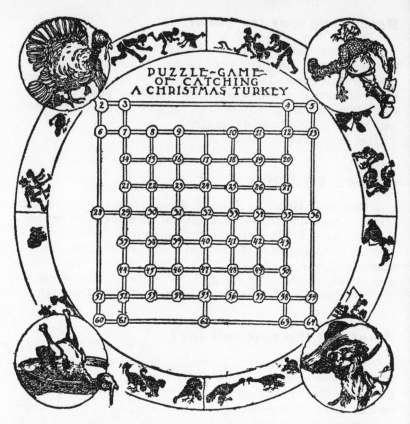

107 *How can the farmer catch the turkey?*

HERE IS a pretty little game as well as a puzzle. Place a counter, supposed to be a turkey, on cell No. 7, and another counter, to represent the farmer, on cell No. 58. One player moves the turkey, the other player moves the farmer. They play alternately, moving their piece in any direction in a straight line, as far as they please. But if a piece stops on a row guarded by the other man, or if it passes over a row so guarded, it can be captured. For example, if the turkey moves first from cell 7 to cell 52, it can immediately be captured by the farmer. And if the farmer moves first from 58 to 4, he can be captured by the turkey at cell 12 because he crossed a row guarded by the turkey. The object of the game is to capture your opponent.

Regardless of who moves first, the farmer can always capture the turkey. What strategy should he follow in order to win?

For a second puzzle, start as before with the turkey on 7 and the farmer on 58. The turkey does not move. How can the farmer capture it in twenty-four moves that take him once and once only over every cell on the board? It is quite a difficult problem.

The Diamond Thief

IN ONE of Dumas' stories about noted criminals, mention is made of a certain jeweler who robbed many ladies of distinction of their finest gems. His method was to substitute imitations or to change the positions of the stones so that a few missing stones would not be detected.

To illustrate the clever rascal's mode of procedure, consider the above picture of an antique pin containing twenty-five diamonds. The lady who owned it had been accustomed to count down from the top to the center, then continue the count either to the left, right, or on down to the bottom. In all three cases the count was exactly thirteen.

This lady made the grave mistake of permitting the jeweler (referred to above) to repair her pin. She showed him her method of counting the gems, and when the pin was returned to her, the jeweler politely counted them again for her. For many years the lady continued to count the diamonds in the same way, always counting thirteen in the three different ways. Yet two of her finest diamonds had been purloined! How did the notorious jeweler rearrange the gems so as to conceal his crime?

109 *Cut the pieces to make a square.*

WHEN MRS. DEACON WHITE bought a piece of linoleum, a little triangular piece was thrown in for nothing. With the good deacon's assistance, she is trying to plan how to cut the two pieces so the parts can be fitted together to make a perfect square. It can be done by cutting the large square into as few as three pieces and the triangle into only two pieces. A pretty geometrical principle is involved that you could not learn at college.

110 *Red Bananas*

"HOW IS IT," said Mrs. O'Neill to Clancy, the mathematical policeman, "that when I buy yellow bananas at thirty cents a bunch and the same number of red ones at forty cents a bunch, I get two more bunches than I would get if I divided the same amount of money evenly between yellow and red bunches?"

"What amount of money?" asked Clancy.

"That's what I want you to tell me," replied Mrs. O'Neill.

THE MONKEY'S PUZZLE

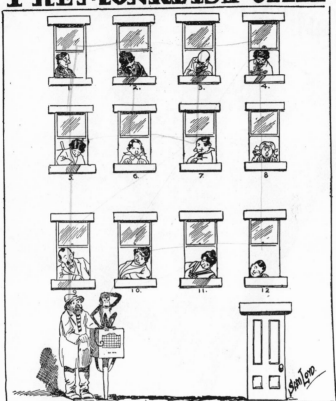

1 What is Jocko's shortest route?

TONY'S ORGAN is sadly out of tune, but his staying powers are inexhaustible, and nothing short of a contribution from each person shown in the picture will bribe him to cease grinding and move on to other quarters.

Now that his audience is ready to capitulate, can you show Jocko the shortest possible route by which he can move from window to window with his little tin cup to collect his dues? The monkey must start from his present position and end his tour by resting on his master's shoulders.

112 *Solve the puzzle in the fewest moves.*

DURING EVERY presidential election I have issued puzzles for campaign purposes, large quantities of which have scattered all over the country. The above picture shows a puzzle that I created as a souvenir of the 1908 election. At the time it caused something of a furor.

Each man on the checkerboard is a candidate for the presidency. The object is to remove eight men, leaving one man on the center square. This is to be done in the fewest possible number of moves. A move consists of (1) moving a man to any adjacent square, up and down, left and right, or diagonally; (2) jumping a man as in checkers except that the jump can also be up and down, left and right, or diagonally. The jumped man is then removed. To work on the puzzle, put buttons or coins on the eight men.

Here is a specimen solution in ten moves: (1) Fairbanks jumps La Follette; (2) Taft jumps Hughes; (3) Johnson jumps Knox; (4) Taft jumps Johnson; (5) Cannon jumps Taft; (6) Cannon jumps Gray; (7) Fairbanks jumps Cannon; (8) Bryan jumps Fairbanks; (9) Bryan moves diagonally down and to the right; (10) Bryan moves to center square. See if you can solve the puzzle in fewer moves.

3 *Chick to Egg*

How would you cut this little chicken into two pieces that can be fitted to form a perfect egg.

IN PUZZLELAND

KING PUZZLEPATE PLAYS· BUNGALOSE·
CRAPS·WITH·THE WILD·MAN·FROM·BORNEO.

109778

114 *How does the wild man score five?*

KING PUZZLEPATE is shown playing a game of Bungalose craps with the wild man from Borneo. In this game, a die is tossed in the air; then the player adds the number that turns up to the number on any one of the four sides. His opponent then scores the total of the remaining three sides. The number on the bottom of the die is never counted. It is a simple game, although mathematicians differ about the exact advantage that the tosser of the die has over his opponent. The sketch shows the wild man making a throw that resulted in the King beating him by five points. The puzzle is to tell what number must have turned up on the die.

Princess Enigma is keeping a tally of the wild man's winnings, and when you see this number translated into Bungalose it will look still larger. The wild men of Borneo, as we all know, have but three fingers on each hand, so they have learned to reckon by the sextimal notation which does not make use of 7, 8, 9, or 10 as in our decimal system. Therefore, as a pretty problem in elementary arithmetic, we ask our puzzlists to translate 109,778 into the Bungalose notation so that the wild man will know just how many gold pieces he has won.

Cut the board to make a square.

THE CARPENTER has a piece of board that contains exactly 81 square inches. The little square piece projecting at the top is one inch on the side. It is attached to a square containing 16 square inches, in turn attached to a larger square of 64 square inches, making 81 square inches altogether. The carpenter wants to make a nine-by-nine square shutter for his window. How can he divide the board into the smallest number of pieces that will fit together to make this square?

Twenty Pieces of Candy

TOMMY, WILLIE, Maggie, and Ann bought twenty pieces of candy for twenty cents. A piece of fudge costs four cents, gum drops are four for a penny, and chocolate drops are two for a penny. How many of each did the children buy?

Puzzling Partnerships

117 *How many fish did each boy catch?*

HERE IS a curious little fishing puzzle that yields readily to experimental methods, although some mathematicians may find it difficult to grasp the situation. Five boys whom we will designate as A, B, C, D, and E, went fishing one day. A and B together caught 14 fish, B and C caught 20, C and D 18, D and E 12, while A and E each caught the same number of fish.

The five boys then divided their spoils as follows. C pooled his catch with B and D; then each of them took exactly one third. Each of the other four boys now did exactly the same thing; that is, each pooled his catch with two side partners, and then the fish were divided into thirds. D pooled with C and E, E pooled with D and A, A pooled with E and B, and B pooled with A and C. The division into thirds came out even, in all five cases, so that no fish had to be sliced into fractions. At the end of this procedure, the fish were divided equally among the five boys.

Can you guess how many fish each boy caught?

The outside borders of the clown's box form an irregular hexagon. Can you cut the hexagon into two pieces that will fit together to make a square?

119 *How many pieces can be produced by six cuts?*

AUNT MARY, who runs a boarding house, has asked her chef to show her boarders how to divide a pie into the greatest possible number of pieces with six straight cuts of the knife. What is your guess as to the number?

120 *The Shy Storekeeper*

"GIVE ME three skeins of silk and four of worsted," said little Susie as she placed 31 cents, the correct amount, on the counter.

As the storekeeper went to get the goods, Susie called out, "I've changed my mind. I'll take four skeins of silk and three of worsted."

"You're just one cent shy," remarked the storekeeper as he placed the goods on the counter.

"Oh no," said Susie as she picked up the goods and skipped out of the store. "*You* are just one cent shy!"

What was the price of silk and worsted?

THE CHRISTMAS TURKEY.

21 *What's wrong with this picture?*

THE TURKEY gobbler has led jolly old Santa Claus a
merry chase around the field, as shown by the tracks in the
snow. You can see that they entered from the right side of
the picture and did some lively circling before arriving at
their present position. Our young folks are asked to study
the situation carefully and see if they can find something
that is very strange, from a mathematical point of view,
about this picture. If you find it, can you think of a plausible
explanation, assuming, of course, that the artist didn't make a
mistake?

122 *How can William Tell score 100?*

THE SKETCH shows William Tell, standing thirty-five yards
from the flagpole, about to demonstrate his skill by shooting
at those apples that Tommy Riddles is supporting. Can you
tell which apples he hit in order to make a score of exactly 100?
The same apple may be hit as often as desired. A second question: what is the height of that flagpole?

123 *Tandem Bicycle*

THREE MEN wish to go forty miles on a tandem bicycle
that will carry no more than two at a time while the third
man is walking. One man, call him A, walks at a rate of one
mile in ten minutes, B can walk a mile in fifteen minutes,
and C can walk a mile in twenty minutes. The bicycle travels
at forty miles an hour regardless of which pair is riding it.
What is the shortest time for all three men to make the trip,
assuming, of course, that they use the most efficient method
of combining walking and cycling?

DISPUTED CLAIMS ~ PRIZE PUZZLE ~ BY~ SAM LOYD.

24 *Give the dimensions of the third triangle.*

OUR PICTURE shows an animated dispute between some miners over their respective claims. Each claim has the form of a right-angle triangle. No two are alike in their dimensions, but each has an area of exactly 3,360 square feet.

The sides of one triangle are 140 and 48, and its hypotenuse is 148. A second triangle has sides of 80 and 84, and a hypotenuse of 116. Can you give the dimensions of the third triangle, assuming that its area is the same as the other two and that its three sides are integral? The triangles shown in the sketch have proportions which are not related to the problem.

25 *Cups and Saucers*

MRS. BARGAINHUNTER purchased $1.30 worth of plates at a sale on Saturday, when two cents was marked off every article. She returned the plates on Monday at regular prices, exchanging them for cups and saucers. One plate was worth a cup and saucer, so she came home with sixteen more articles than she had before. Since saucers were worth only three cents, she took ten more saucers than cups.

The puzzle is to tell how many cups Mrs. Bargainhunter could have bought on Saturday with her $1.30.

THE MATHEMATICAL MILKMAN OF PUZZLELAND

126 *Find the proportions of milk and water.*

"IN ONE can I have some pure spring water," explained the milkman to the two schoolboys. "In the other can there is some milk so rich with cream that it is absolutely necessary to dilute it with water to make it wholesome. I do this by first pouring from can A into can B enough liquid to double the contents of B. Then I pour from B to A enough liquid to double A's contents. Finally, I pour from A to B again until B's contents are doubled. I find that each milk can now contains the same amount, and that in B there is one more gallon of water than there is milk. How much water and milk did I start with and how much water and milk is in each can at the finish?"

127 *The Owl Express*

BIG JIM, engineer of the Owl Express, says: "We blew off a cylinder head an hour after leaving the station and had to continue the trip at three fifths of our former speed. This brought us to the next station two hours late. If the accident had occurred fifty miles farther on, the train would have arrived forty minutes sooner."

How far is it between stations?

ANCIENT
ORDER
— OF THE —
IRON CROSS
BY
SAM LOYD

28 *Dissect the cross into pieces that form a square.*

ACCORDING TO legend, Caesar Augustus was riding in his chariot one day when he noticed the one-armed soldier, Titus Livius, begging alms. Caesar stopped to ask the veteran why he had not received the cross of honor and the pension due to soldiers who had lost a limb in honorable service.

"Great Caesar," replied the warrior, "I was but a humble soldier in the ranks, and was doubtless overlooked."

Caesar took the decoration from his own chest and placed it on the soldier. "If you had lost both arms, you would be the founder of a new order."

Hearing this, the soldier promptly drew his sword and by a deft stroke lopped off his other arm!

We will not go into a discussion of the paradoxical features of this exploit, but concern ourselves with the shape of the St. Andrews Cross which Titus is wearing on his chest. The problem is to cut this cross into the fewest number of pieces that will fit together to make a square.

129 *Dividing Apples*

EIGHT CHILDREN divided 32 apples as follows. Ann got
one apple, May two, Jane three, and Kate four. Ned Smith
took as many as his sister, Tom Brown took twice as many
as his sister, Bill Jones three times as many as his sister,
and Jack Robinson four times as many as his sister. The puzzle
is to tell the last names of the four girls.

130 *Marbles for Keeps*

HARRY AND Jim, two rival marble-shooters, each had the
same number of marbles when they started to play for keeps.
Harry won twenty marbles in the first round, but lost two
thirds of his stock in the play-off. This left Jim with four
times as many marbles as Harry.

How many marbles did each boy have when they started
to play?

131 *Mixed Tea*

A HONG KONG shopkeeper sold a popular mixture of two
kinds of tea, one of which cost him five bits per pound and
the other three bits. He mixed up forty pounds, which he
sold for six bits per pound, making a profit of 33 and $\frac{1}{3}$
per cent.

How many pounds of the five-bit tea did he use in the
mixture?

132 *How old is the Boss?*

I SPENT one sixth of my years in the old country as a
boy," remarked the Boss, "one twelfth in the liquor business
in New York and one seventh and five years in politics and
matrimony, which takes me to the time that Jimmy was born.
He was elected alderman four years ago when he was but
half my present age."

How old is the Boss?

33 *Solve Christopher's egg tricks.*

LITTLE TOMMY is calling attention to a couple of egg
puzzles that Christopher Columbus has asked King Puzzlepate
to solve. The first is to place nine eggs on the table in such a
way as to form the greatest possible number of rows, each row
with three eggs in a straight line. The King has succeeded in
getting eight rows, as shown in the picture, but the hen claims
that any smart chicken can do better than that!

The funny old King is now trying to work out the second
puzzle, which is to draw a continuous series of straight lines
that will pass through the centers of all the eggs in the fewest
number of strokes. He has performed the feat in six strokes,
but we take it from Tommy's expression that this is a very
stupid answer. It is an ingenious trick, fully as good if not
better than that of making an egg stand on end, for the per-
petration of which (with an over-ripe egg), the great navi-
gator was loaded with chains.

134 *How much land will a dozen rails enclose?*

THE YOUNG lad in the sketch has just asked Mr. Lincoln how much land can be enclosed by those dozen rails. "That all depends," Mr. Lincoln is saying, "on the length of the rail."

Assume that each rail is sixteen feet long. What is the largest area of land that can be enclosed by the twelve rails? If the rails are arranged in square formation, for example, they will enclose 2,304 square feet of land, but it is possible to do much better than this.

135 *Diminishing Power*

MONSIEUR DE FOIE GRAS, the noted French chauffeur, mentions that on a certain motoring trip his car went 135 miles during the first two hours and 104 miles during the next two hours. Assuming that the power steadily diminished during the four hours so that each hourly run decreased in miles by the same amount, how far did the car travel during each of the four hours?

36 *How close can you come to 82?*

HERE IS a famous problem that I issued in 1882, offering $1,000 as a prize for the best answer. The problem is to arrange the seven digits and the eight dots in such a way that the figures add up to a sum that is as close to 82 as possible. The dots may be used in two ways: (1) as a decimal point, (2) as a symbol for a repeating decimal. For example, the fraction 1/3 may be written .$\dot{3}$. The dot over the 3 indicates that it is repeated endlessly. If a sequence of digits is repeated, then dots are used to mark the beginning and end of the sequence. Thus, the fraction 1/7 may be written .$\dot{1}$42857$\dot{}$.

Out of several million answers, only two were found to be correct.

137 *Time the two skaters.*

TWO GRACEFUL skaters, Jennie and Maude, stood a mile apart on a frozen lake, then each skated directly to the spot where the other had been standing. With the help of a strong wind, Jennie performed the feat two and one-half times faster than Maude and beat her by six minutes. How long did it take each girl to skate the mile?

138 *Polar Bride*

ON A RECENT expedition to the North Pole, a member of the exploring party attempted to capture for himself a bride. Natives of the region all sleep in bearskin sacks, and the custom is for the lovesick swain to creep in and steal the sack containing his prospective mate.

In this case the lover had quite a distance to journey, but he made the trip there at a rate of five miles per hour, and returned with his burden at a rate of three miles per hour, taking exactly seven hours for the entire round trip. When he opened the sack to show the prize to his shipmates, he found that by mistake he had carried away the girl's grandfather.

The story is no doubt exaggerated, but will our experts tell us just how far the explorer traveled on this memorable journey?

39 *Find the approach speed of two goats.*

"I ONCE witnessed a duel to the death between two goats," writes Professor Blumgarten, "which introduces a pretty mathematical problem. A neighbor of mine had a goat that held the undisputed championship of the rocks for several seasons; then someone introduced to the area a new goat that was three pounds heavier. The first goat weighed 54 pounds, the newcomer 57.

"To all appearances, the goats were living harmoniously. Then one day the lighter of the two stationed himself at the top of a steep pathway, and from that point hurled defiance at his rival. The rival started up the hill on a run and was met by the other goat who had the advantage of running downhill. Sad to tell, both goats were killed by the collision.

"Now comes the curious feature of the problem. George Abercrombie, who wrote a considerable work on the raising of goats, says: 'By repeated experiments I have found that the strength of a blow equal to the momentum of 30 pounds falling 20 feet will just break the skull of a goat, so as to kill it.' Assuming that this is correct, what must have been the minimum approach velocity of those two goats in order to break one another's skulls?"

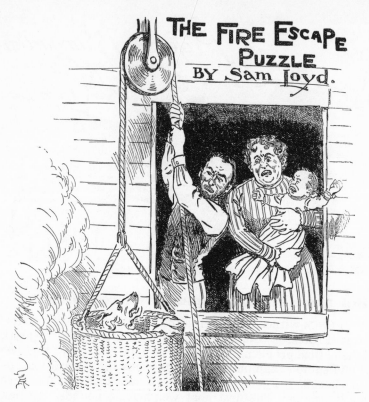

140 *Lower the family in the fewest moves.*

THE BINKS patent fire escape is merely a rope that runs over a pulley with a large basket at each end of the rope. When one bucket goes down, the other comes up. By putting an object in one basket to act as a counterbalance, a heavier object can then be lowered in the other basket. The inventor says that his device should be placed outside every sleeping room in the world. It was tried at one of our hotels, but delinquent guests had such a way of decamping during the night with their worldly possessions that the scheme no longer finds favor with hotel owners.

The sketch above shows a Binks elevator outside the window of a fashionable summer hotel. Nothing weighing more than thirty pounds can be lowered safely in one basket while the other basket is empty, and thirty pounds is the safety limit of difference between the two baskets when each is carrying a weight.

When a fire occurred at the hotel one night, all the guests escaped in safety except the night watchman and his family. They could not be aroused until all ways of escape were cut off except for the Binks elevator. The watchman weighed 90 pounds, his wife weighed 210 pounds, the dog weighed 60 pounds, and the baby weighed 30 pounds.

Each basket is large enough to hold all four, but no weights are to be used in the baskets — only the man, wife, dog, and baby are involved in the escape. It is assumed that neither dog nor baby is capable of climbing in or out of a basket without the assistance of the man or his wife. What is the most efficient way in which all four can get down safely?

1 *Aesop's Eagle*

AMONG THE fables of Aesop is the story of the ambitious eagle who resolved to fly to the sun. Every morning when the sun rose in the east, the eagle would fly toward it until noon; then as the sun began to move down toward the west, the eagle would reverse his direction and fly westward on its hopeless chase. Just as the sun disappeared below the western horizon, the eagle would find itself back at the original starting point.

It is a good story, but Aesop's mathematics are badly out of gear. During the morning part of the eagle's flight, the bird and sun are advancing toward each other, whereas during the afternoon flight, the eagle and sun are moving in the same direction. It is clear that the afternoon flight will be the longer one, carrying the eagle farther west each day.

Let us assume that the bird starts its tour from the dome of the Capitol Building at Washington, D.C., where the earth's circumference is 19,500 miles. The eagle flies at a height from the earth's surface that does not materially affect the distance, and each day it ends its flight 500 miles west of the point from which it started in the morning.

How many days will it take the eagle to reach the Capitol's dome after having made a complete westward circuit of the earth?

142 *How many triangles are on the seal?*

LITTLE TOMMY RIDDLES announces that King Puzzlepate
and Princess Enigma are investigating the secrets of the
famous seal of King Solomon ,which is engraved on the royal
tomb. The King is trying to figure out just how many different
equilateral triangles can be found in the design. What is your
guess?

143 *The Hare and the Tortoise*

A SPORTIVE young hare and a tortoise raced in opposite
directions around a circular track that was 100 yards in
diameter. They started at the same spot, but the hare did not
move until the tortoise had a start of one eighth of the
distance (that is, the circumference of the circle). The hare
held such a poor opinion of the other's racing ability that
he sauntered along, nibbling the grass until he met the tortoise. At this point the hare had gone one sixth of the
distance. How many times faster than he went before must
the hare now run in order to win the race?

4 *Solve the Swiss miss's flag problems.*

THIS PRETTY Swiss miss is extremely clever at working geometrical cutting puzzles. She has discovered a way of cutting the piece of red wall paper in her right hand into two pieces that will fit together to form the Swiss flag she is holding in her left hand. The white cross in the center of the flag is actually a hole in the paper. The cutting must follow the lines ruled on the paper.

For a second puzzle, the Swiss girl asks you to cut the flag in her left hand into two pieces that will fit together to make a rectangle of five-by-six units.

Someone once asked the Swiss girl how to make a Maltese cross and she replied, "Pull its tail!"

145 *How much wire will it take?*

To SHOW how good puzzle ideas may be picked up from time to time "as we journey by the way," I will give a little problem that I was called upon to tackle the other day. I found an electrician, who had invented some kind of switchboard, trying to work out the most economical method of stringing a fine copper wire through all the contact points on his board. The board was an elaborate affair, consisting of several hundred points, but since 64 is sufficient to illustrate our problem, only an eight-by-eight section of the board is shown above.

The problem is to find the shortest length of wire that will go from point B to the center of the little square marked A. The wire must touch the centers of all 64 little squares. Each square is one inch wide, and they are spaced so their centers are three inches apart. Each time a wire turns a corner, it is necessary to wind it around a corner of the square, an operation that uses two inches of wire. No diagonal connections are permitted.

Assuming that two inches of wire are used in going from B to the center of the nearest little square, can you determine the shortest length of wire required to go from B to A?

How far does the courier travel?

AN ANCIENT problem, to be found in many old puzzle books, concerns an army fifty miles long. As the army marches forward at a constant rate, a courier starts at the rear of the army, rides forward to deliver a message to the front, then returns to his position at the rear. He arrives back exactly at the time that the army completed an advance of fifty miles. How far altogether did the courier travel?

If the army were stationary, he would clearly have to travel fifty miles forward and the same distance back. But because the army is advancing, he must go more than fifty miles to the front, and on his return trip he will travel less than fifty miles because the rear of the army is advancing toward him. It is assumed, of course, that the courier always rides at a constant speed.

A more difficult puzzle is created by the following extension of the theme. A square army, fifty miles long by fifty miles wide, advances fifty miles at a constant rate while a courier starts at the middle of the rear and makes a complete circuit around the army and back to his starting point. The courier's speed is constant, and he completes his circuit just as the army completes its advance. How far does the courier travel?

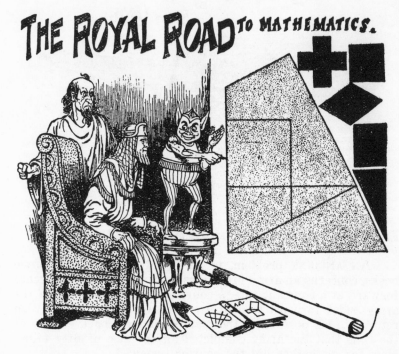

147 *Form the six figures with the five pieces.*

BEPPO, THE court jester, is explaining to King Ptolemy how he can mark off the trapezium into five parts that can be used for six wonderful puzzles. Trace the trapezium on a sheet of cardboard, cut out the five pieces, then see if you can put them together to form:

1. A square.
2. A Greek cross.
3. A diamond.
4. A rectangle.
5. A right-angle triangle.
6. The original trapezium.

The five other figures are shown in small silhouettes so that you can see how they are shaped. All five pieces must be utilized in producing each of the six patterns.

MOTHER'S JAM PUZZLE

8 *How much does each jar hold?*

MRS. HUBBARD has invented a clever system for keeping tabs on her jars of blackberry jam. She has arranged the jars in her cupboard so that she has twenty quarts of jam on each shelf. The jars are in three sizes. Can you tell how much each size contains?

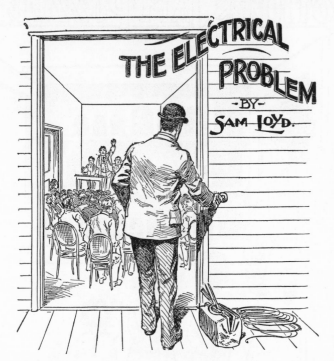

149 *What is the shortest path for the wire?*

DURING A recent county political convention, an electrician was hired to install an annunciator at the back of the meeting hall. It was to be connected to a push button at the front door, so that the managers could notify the long-winded orators when to ring off. The length of wire required for this job was a topic of debate among the workmen, and the question was referred to me.

The hall, as shown in the above sketch, was just 12 feet wide by 12 feet high, and 30 feet in length. The wire was to go from the annunciator, three feet from the ceiling at the center of the back wall, to a push button three feet from the floor at the center of the front wall. The wire can be strung along walls, ceiling, or floor. The problem is to determine the shortest possible route that the wire can take. The thickness of the wall at the push button need not be considered.

Puppies and Rats

A SMALL merchant of Canton bought a certain number of fat puppies and half that many pairs of rats. He paid two bits each for the puppy dogs and the same price for each pair of rats. Then he sold the animals for prices that were an advance of ten per cent over what he paid for them.

After the Chinese merchant had disposed of all but seven animals, he found that he had taken in an amount of money exactly equal to what he had originally paid for all the animals. His profit, therefore, was represented by the retail value of the seven remaining animals.

What are those seven animals worth at the merchant's retail prices?

Division of Capital

IN THE old firm of Brown and Jones, Brown had 1 and ½ times as much capital invested in the business as Jones. It was decided to admit Robinson into the firm upon the payment of $2,500 which was to be divided between Brown and Jones in such a way that the interests of the three partners would be equal. How should the $2,500 be divided?

Mrs. Hogan's Clothes Line

MRS. HOGAN bought a new 100-foot clothes line, sharing the cost with her friend, Mary O'Neill. Since Mrs. Hogan paid the larger part of the bill, one piece was only five sevenths the length of the other.

How long was each piece?

Jones' Cows

FARMER JONES sold a pair of cows for $210. On one he made a profit of ten per cent and on the other he lost ten per cent. Altogether he made a profit of five per cent. How much did each cow originally cost him?

154 *Find the quickest route to the flag.*

THIS LITTLE problem involving a cross-country steeple-chase should interest racing fans as well as puzzlists. It appears that near the end of a well-contested race, when there remained only 1 and ¾ miles yet to go, the leaders were so closely bunched together that victory turned upon the selection of the best shortcut to the home flag. The sketch shows the judges' stand at the far end of a rectangular field bounded by a road that is a mile long on one side and three quarters of a mile on the other.

By the road, therefore, the distance to the home flag is 1 and ¾ miles, which all the horses can run in three minutes. They are at liberty, however, to cut across lots wherever they wish, but over the rough ground they cannot go so fast. In this case, the ground of the rectangular lot will cause them to lose 25 per cent of their speed.

In order to finish the race in the shortest possible time, at what point along that mile of road should a horse leap the stone fence and head straight for the home flag?

5 *Increase the even rows.*

THESE JOLLY friars have placed ten coins, one coin to a cell, so that they form ten rows, each row containing an even number of coins. Rows may be counted horizontally, vertically, or diagonally. The puzzle is to rearrange the coins to form the largest possible number of even rows.

6 *The Shady Grove*

MR. AND MRS. SMITH were about to purchase a suburban house. "If you give me three quarters of your money," said Mr. Smith, "I can combine it with my money and have just enough to buy this $5,000 house. You will have just enough money left to buy the shady grove and running stream in back of the house."

"No, no," replied his better half. "Give me two thirds of your money and I will combine it with mine and have just enough to buy the house, and you will have just enough left to purchase the grove with the babbling brook."

Can you figure out the value of the shady grove with its never-failing stream?

157 *Find the shortest path that catches all the mice.*

DICK WHITTINGTON has trained his cat to go from mouse A (upper left corner) to mouse Z (lower right corner) by the shortest route along the black lines that will enable the cat to catch all the mice.

While the King tries to puzzle out this problem, Dick is pointing out the clock on the Tower of London and asking: "If it takes six seconds for the clock to strike six, how long will it take the clock to strike eleven?"

158 *Horse Trade*

FOR SOME reason or other I never was much of a success as a horse trader. I bought a bronco down in Texas for $26. After paying for his keep for a while, I sold him for $60. That looked like a profitable deal, but considering the cost of his keep, I found I had lost an amount equal to half of what I paid for him plus one fourth of the cost of his keep. Can you figure out how much I lost?

9 *Arrange the eight bars to make three squares of equal size.*

BY USING eight wooden bars, Bo-Peep has constructed two square folds for her two toy lambs. An admirer has just presented her with a third lamb, so she wants to rearrange the bars to make three square folds.

Cut eight narrow strips of cardboard, making four of them twice as long as the others, as shown at the bottom of the picture. The puzzle is this: arrange the eight strips on a flat surface in such a manner that they form three squares, all the same size.

0 *Quick Deal*

WHILE THE suburban boom is on, we will take occasion to tell how a real-estate speculator stopped off at a wrong station and, having a couple of hours to wait for the next train, made a quick and profitable deal. He bought a piece of land for $243 which he divided into equal lots, then sold them at $18 per lot, cleaning up the whole transaction before his train arrived. His profit on the deal was exactly equal to what six of the lots originally cost him.

How many lots were in that piece of land?

161 *Separate the boys and girls.*

THE EIGHT street urchins in the above picture are standing so that boys and girls alternate along the line. The problem is to rearrange them so that the four soldiers are on one
side and the four Red Cross lassies are on the other, with all
eight standing close together as before. This must be done in
four moves only, each move consisting of shifting the position
of one pair of adjacent children.

A good way to work on the problem is to put a penny on
each boy and a dime on each girl; then by shifting the coins
two at a time, try to bring all the pennies to one side and the
dimes to the other side in just four moves. Remember: the
shifted coins must be adjacent pairs, and you cannot reverse
their order in the shifting. For instance, you can shift D and
E (the letters are on the hats) to the left end of the line, but
in doing so you cannot turn them around so that E is to the
left of D.

PUZZLE OF AN ECCENTRIC WILL

52 *Guess the last names of each heir.*

WHEN CAPTAIN JOHN SMITH died at Gloucester in 1803, a respected and worthy citizen, he left the proceeds of his successful ventures in the slave and smuggling traffic to his nine heirs. The heirs consisted of a son, his wife, and child; a daughter, her husband, and child; and a stepson who also had a wife and child.

The captain stipulated in his will that each husband would receive more than his wife, and each wife more than her child. The difference in each of these six cases was to be the same amount. That is, each husband's sum exceeded his wife's by the same amount, and this same amount also represented the difference between each wife's sum and that of her child. The money consisted entirely of one-dollar bills. Each heir received his money in a package of sealed envelopes, each envelope containing just as many dollar bills as there were envelopes in the package.

It was also stated in the will that "Mary and Sarah together get just as much as Tom and Bill together, while Ned, Bill and Mary together get $299 more than Hank. In consideration of the needy circumstances of the Jones family, they get altogether over one third more than the Browns."

The portraits shown above give no indications of the relative ages of the nine heirs, but from the data in Captain Smith's will, our puzzlists should have no trouble in guessing the family surnames of each heir and the amount of money each received.

THE FAMOUS HOT CROSS BUN PUZZLE

HOT X BUNS

3 *How many buns did each child get?*

MANY OF those jingling old nursery melodies conceal riddles or puzzles that are worth the investigation of children of
a larger growth. Take, for example, the cry of the Hot-Cross-
Bun Man:

> Hot-cross buns, hot-cross buns,
>   One a penny, two a penny,
> Hot-cross buns.
>   If your daughters don't like them
> Give them to your sons!
>   Two a penny, three a penny,
> Hot-cross buns.
>   I had as many daughters as I had sons,
> So I gave them seven pennies
>   To buy their hot-cross buns.

The inference is clear that there are three sizes of buns:
one for a penny, two for a penny, and three for a penny. There
were just as many boys as girls, and they were given seven
pennies altogether. Assuming that each child got exactly the
same number and kinds of buns, can you tell how many buns
each received?

4 *Bill Sykes*

I ASKED Bill Sykes if he wanted to work and he replied,
"Why should I work?"

"To earn money," I said.

"What's the use of earning money?" he asked.

"To save it up," I replied.

"But what do I want to save money for?"

"So that when you grow old you can rest," said I.

"But I am growing old as fast as I wish now," says he,
"and what's the use of working to rest when I can begin to
rest right now."

I failed to convince him, but I did get him to agree to try
working for thirty days at $8 a day, although it was stipu-
lated that he would forfeit $10 for every day that he idled.
At the end of the month, neither he nor his employer owed
the other anything, which convinced Bill of the folly of labor.

How many days did Bill work and how many days did he
loaf?

165 *Cover all points but one.*

AMONG THE great men of our time, noted for overcoming
early obstacles and battling their way to success, the late
Henry George should be accorded well deserved prominence.
By the profound study of taxation, the author of *Progress and
Poverty* became so familiar with every phase of his subject
that he was absolutely invulnerable in debate. We often discussed the problems pertaining to the single tax, and I became
convinced that there would be no competent successor to take
up his mantle.

At one time, when we used to meet almost daily at the Press
Club, Mr. George had been tantalizing me with some of his
mighty problems on political economy. I retaliated by offering

this puzzle of my own, built on the principle of a familiar puzzle involving counters and the points of a star.

The object of the puzzle is to place twelve counters on the thirteen spots of the diagram. Each counter must first be placed on an empty spot, then moved along either of the two lines to another empty spot and left there. For example, you might place the first counter on spot No. 2 and move it to No. 4 or to No. 13. Once a counter has been moved it must remain fixed and cannot move again, and no counter can be placed (before or after moving it) on a spot already occupied by a counter.

After you have learned how to place all twelve counters on the diagram, you are ready to try the second and more difficult part of the puzzle. Select an English word of twelve letters. Write a letter on each counter; then take them in regular order, beginning with the first letter of the word, and see if you can place them on the diagram so that the word will spell correctly as you read the letters clockwise around the circle.

Henry George was greatly pleased with the puzzle and paid me the equivocal compliment of saying it was "the brightest thing I had ever originated." See if you can find a good twelve-letter word which can be readily placed upon the points.

6 *Casey's Cow*

"SOME COWS have more sense than the average man," said Farmer Casey. "My old brindle was standing on a bridge the other day, five feet from the middle of the bridge, placidly looking into the water. Suddenly she spied the lightning express, just twice the length of the bridge away from the nearest end of the bridge, coming toward her at a 90-mile an hour clip.

"Without wasting a moment in idle speculation, the cow made a dash toward the advancing train and saved herself by the narrow margin of one foot. If she had followed the human instinct of running away from the train at the same speed, three inches of her rear would have been caught on the bridge!"

What is the length of the bridge and the gait of Casey's cow?

SOLUTIONS

Answer 1

[Sam Loyd answers this famous problem incorrectly by saying that as the monkey climbs the rope, he will fall with rapidly increasing speed. The correct answer is that regardless of how the monkey climbs—fast, slow, or by jumps—monkey and weight always remain opposite. The monkey cannot get above or below the weight even by letting go of the rope, dropping, and grabbing the rope again.

Lewis Carroll's statement on the problem is to be found in his *Diary*, volume 2, page 505, and the problem is discussed in *The Life and Letters of Lewis Carroll*, by S. D. Collingwood, page 317; *A Handbook of the Literature of the Reverend C. L. Dodgson*, by Sidney Williams and Falconer Madan, page xvii; and *The Lewis Carroll Picture Book*, by S. D. Collingwood, page 267. The last reference presents a British reverend's defense of the view that the weight remains stationary. For a sound analysis of the problem see the letter by A. G. Samuelson in *Scientific American*, June, 1956, page 19.—M.G.]

Answer 2

The hammock can be divided with twelve cuts as shown below.

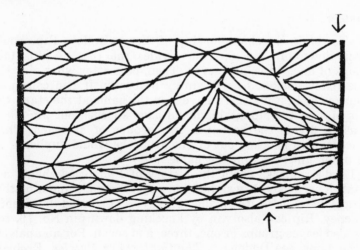

Answer 3

The cook bought sixteen eggs, but the grocer threw in two extra eggs, making eighteen in all.

Answer 4

It is possible to divide a pancake into 29 pieces by seven straight cuts.

The right-triangle has integral sides of 47, 1,104 and 1,105. Strange that the fool should have hit upon 47, which has but one answer in whole numbers. There would have been ten answers if he had said 48 rails.

I really blush to give the fool's answer to the question of why the sword is curved. It is curved so that it will fit its scabbard!

Answer 5

The milkman delivered 32 quarts of pure milk on the first street, 24 quarts on the second, 18 on the third, and 13 and 1/2 on the fourth, making 87 and 1/2 quarts altogether.

Answer 6

To retain the championship of Sleepy Hollow, Rip should knock down pin No. 6. This divides the row of pins into groups of one, three, and seven. Then, no matter what play the little fellow makes, he will surely be beaten if Rip continues to make the best plays. To have won the game at the start, the little Man-of-the-Mountain should have knocked out pin No. 7 so as to divide the row into two groups of six each. Then whatever Rip knocked out of one group he would duplicate on the other until he won the game.

[Loyd's remarks about the history of *Kugelspiel* should not be taken seriously. It was just his way of introducing a mathematical version of the game of kayles, invented by Henry Dudeney. Rip can also win by knocking down pin No. 10, for this also leaves groups of one, three, and seven. For an analysis of the game, see Dudeney's *The Canterbury Puzzles*, Problem No. 73, and W. Rouse Ball's *Mathematical Recreations.*—M.G.]

Answer 7

Pat's pigsty puzzle can be solved only by the clever expedient of nesting the pens, one inside of another, as below:

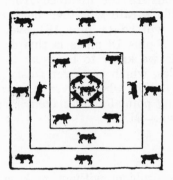

Answer 8

The path shown below requires only fourteen right-angle turns.

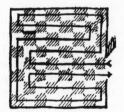

Answer 9

The Jones boys sold 220 more papers than the Smith boys. The original number of papers was 1,020.

Answer 10

Mary's age is 27 years and 6 months.

Answer 11

The distance between Pleasantville and Joytown is 126 miles. [Let x be the distance from the meeting point to Pleasantville, and x plus 18 the distance from Joytown to the meeting spot. Willie's rate will then be x over 13 and 1/2, and Dusty's rate will be (x plus 18) over 24. The time it took Willie to go x plus 18 miles is this distance divided by Willie's rate. This we know to be equal to the time it took Dusty to go x miles, which is x over Dusty's rate. This leads to a quadratic equation which gives x a value of 54 miles, making the meeting point 54 miles from Pleasantville and 72 miles from Joytown.—M.G.]

Answer 12

To solve this problem without making use of *pi*, it is necessary to recall Archimedes' great discovery that the volume of a sphere is two thirds the volume of a cylindrical box into which the sphere exactly fits. The ball of wire has a diameter of 24 inches, so its volume is the same as that of a cylinder with a height of 16 inches and a base diameter of 24 inches.

Now wire is simply an extended cylinder. How many pieces of wire, each 16 inches high and one hundredth of an inch in diameter, are equal in volume to the 16-inch high cylinder with a base diameter of 24 inches? Areas of circles are in the same proportion to each other as the squares of their diameters. The square of 1/100 is 1/10,000 and the square of 24 is 576, so we conclude that the cylinder is equal in volume to 5,760,000 of the 16-inch-long wires. The total length of the wire, therefore, is 5,760,000 times 16, or 92,160,000 inches. This reduces to 1,484 miles and 2,880 feet.

Answer 13

After 12 o'clock the two hands first point in opposite directions at 32 and 8/11 minutes after 12, and at intervals of 1 hour, 5 and 5/11 minutes thereafter. The position of the second hand shows that the clock must have been struck by the bullet at 21 and 9/11 minutes (49 and 1/11 seconds) after 10 o'clock.

Answer 14

When the ferry boats meet at point X (see above diagram) they are 720 yards from one shore. The combined distance that both have traveled is equal to the width of the river. When they reach the opposite shore, the combined distance is equal to twice the width of the river. On the return trip they meet at point Z after traveling a combined distance of three times the width of the river, so each boat has gone three times as far as they had gone when they first met.

At the first meeting, one boat had gone 720 yards, so when it reaches Z it must have gone three times that distance, or 2,160 yards. As the diagram shows, this distance is 400 yards more than the river's width, so all the mathematical work we are obliged to do is to deduct 400 from 2,160 to get the river's width. It is 1,760 yards which is exactly one mile.

The amount of time each ship consumed at the landing does not affect the problem.

Answer 15

The nine matches are placed so as to form the letters of the word TEN, and the six are arranged to spell the word NIX.

Answer 16

From the facts given we can conclude that Jack eats lean pork at a rate of 1 barrel in 10 weeks, therefore he would finish the half-barrel of lean in 5 weeks. During this same period, his wife (who eats fat at a rate of 1 barrel in 12 weeks) would consume 5/12 of a barrel of fat. This would leave 1/12 of a barrel of fat for both of them to eat at a rate of 1 barrel in 60 days. They would finish the fat in 5 days, so the total amount of time would be 35 days plus 5 days, or 40 days altogether.

Answer 17

Because the miser could divide each type of coin evenly into four, five, and six parts, he must have had not less than sixty coins of each type, making a total of $2,100.

Answer 18

[Loyd's six-piece solution is shown below. For a completely different solution, in ten pieces, consult Henry Dudeney's *The Canterbury Puzzles,* Problem 37.—M.G.]

Answer 19

Jennie's trick was to move that one ring from the left to the extreme right as shown.

Answer 20

The various workmen charged as follows:

Paper hanger	$ 200
Painter	900
Plumber	800
Electrician	300
Carpenter	3,000
Mason	2,300

[For an interesting trick with a dollar bill, based on the formula for solving problems of this type, see page 52 of my book *Mathematics, Magic and Mystery.*—M.G.]

Answer 21

The time is 18 and 6/13 minutes past eight, which may also be expressed as 18 minutes, 27 and 9/13 seconds.

Answer 22

[Jack's total time up and down hill is exactly 6.3 minutes or 6 minutes and 18 seconds. The problem is handled algebraically by letting $2x$ stand for Jack's speed up, $3x$ for his speed down, $2y$ for Jill's speed up, $3y$ for her speed down. Equate Jack's time until he meets Jill with Jill's time until she meets Jack. Then equate Jack's total time, plus one-half minute, with Jill's total time. The two simultaneous equations can now be solved for x and y.—M.G.]

Answer 23

Call one ten-gallon milk can A and the other B, then proceed as follows:

Fill 5 pail from can A.
Fill 4 pail from 5 pail, leaving 1 quart in 5 pail.
Empty 4 pail into can A.
Pour the quart from 5 pail into 4 pail.
Fill 5 pail from can A.
Fill 4 pail from 5 pail, leaving 2 quarts in 5 pail.
Empty 4 pail into can A.
Fill 4 pail from can B.

Pour from 4 pail into can A until A is filled, leaving 2 quarts in 4 pail.

Each pail now holds 2 quarts, can A is full, and can B is missing 4 quarts.

Answer 24

Assume that cars and engines are labeled ABCDEFGHI from left to right. E is the broken-down engine and F the engine that does all the work. The problem is solved in 31 engine reversals as follows:

Engine F moves straight to engine E, hooks to E, and pulls it to section D of switch. (1 reversal)

F goes through the switch, hooks to D, pulls D to section D of the switch, at the same time pushing E to right. (3 reversals)

F goes through switch again, hooks to C, pulls C to section D, pushing D to right. (3 reversals)

F goes through switch, hooks to B, pulls B to section D, pushing C to right. (3 reversals)

F goes through switch, hooks to A, pulls A to section D, pushing B to right. (3 reversals)

F goes through switch, then moves to right, pushing A against B. Cars ABCDEG are hooked together. (3 reversals)

F draws ABCDEG to left, then pushes G to section A of switch. (2 reversals)

F pulls ABCDE to left, then pushes them to right. (2 reversals)

F moves alone to left, backs up and hooks to G, pulls G to left. (3 reversals)

F moves right, pushing G against A. G is hooked to A, then F pulls entire string of cars and engine to left. (2 reversals)

F backs H and I to sections A and B of the switch, pulls GABCDE to left, then pushes all of them to right. (3 reversals)

F pulls G to left, backs up and hooks G to H, pulls GHI to left and proceeds on its way. This leaves the other train, with its cars in the same order behind the engine as before, on the straight track to the right of the switch. (3 reversals)

Answer 25

The cheapest way to make an endless chain out of the six five-link pieces is to open up all five links of one piece, then use them for joining the remaining five pieces into an endless chain. The cost for this would be $1.30, which is 20 cents cheaper than the cost of a new endless chain.

Answer 26

The first gingerbread problem is answered as follows:

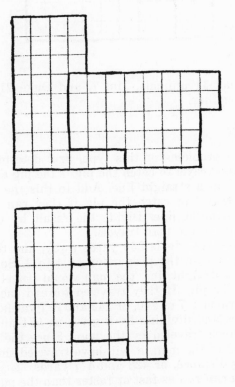

[The best solution I can find for the second problem, which is not answered in the *Cyclopedia,* is shown below. Each piece contains twenty-nine small squares. If any reader can improve on this, I will be pleased to hear from him.—M.G.]

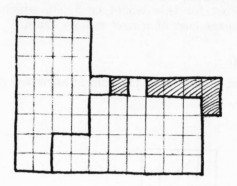

Answer 27

Hank had 11 animals, Jim 7, and Duke 21, making 39 animals altogether.

Answer 28

To solve problems of this type, first determine how far the man would travel to catch the pig if the pig and man both ran forward on a straight line. Add to this the distance the man would travel to catch the pig if they ran toward each other on a straight line. Divide the result by two and you have the distance the man travels.

In this case, the pig is 250 yards away, and the speeds of man and pig are in the proportion of 4 to 3. So if both ran forward on a straight line, the man would travel 1,000 yards to overtake the pig. If they traveled toward each other, the man would travel 4/7 of 250, or 142 and 6/7 yards. Adding the two distances and dividing by 2 gives us 571 and 3/7 yards for the distance traveled by the man. Since the pig runs at 3/4 the speed of the man, it will have traveled three quarters of the man's distance, or 428 and 4/7 yards.

[If the pig can run as fast or faster than the man, it is easy to see from Loyd's rule that it can never be caught. But if the man's speed exceeds that of the pig, the pig can always be captured. The man's path forms one of the simplest of "pursuit curves," the study of which forms an interesting branch of what one might call "recreational calculus."—M.G.]

Answer 29

Forty years ago Biddy was 18, which makes her 58 now.

Answer 30

The key words are "PEACH BLOWS" (a popular variety of potato). Number these letters from 1 to 0, and you will find that all the words on the sign, when properly translated, will add to "ALL WOOL," which is, to say the least, a remarkable coincidence.

Answer 31

Josiah and Mariah must have had 300 chickens with feed enough to last 60 days.

Answer 32

The ball would travel a distance of 218.77777 plus feet, or very close to 218 feet, 9 and 1/3 inches.

Answer 33

The route shown below will take Clancy past *all* the houses.

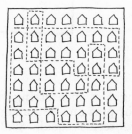

Answer 34

(1) There are an infinite number of ways to cut a Greek cross into four pieces that will make a perfect square. The illustration below shows one of them. It is a striking fact that any two straight cuts made parallel to the two cuts here shown will achieve the same result. The resulting four pieces can always be formed into a square!

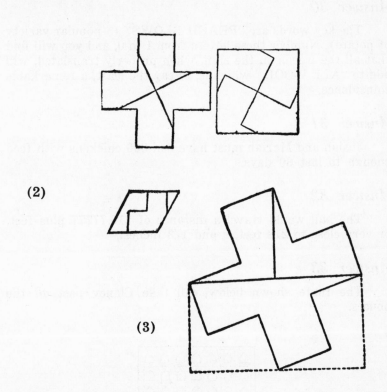

(2)

(3)

Answer 35

If the lady bought x shoe strings then she must have bought $4x$ packages of pins and $8x$ handkerchiefs. The sum of the squares of these terms equals $3.24, which gives x a value of 2. So the lady bought 2 shoe strings, 8 packages of pins, and 16 handkerchiefs.

Answer 36

The flask and brush can be transposed in sixteen moves as follows:

1.	Flask	10.	Pepperbox
2.	Brush	11.	Iron
3.	Iron	12.	Flask
4.	Flask	13.	Mousetrap
5.	Pepperbox	14.	Iron
6.	Mousetrap	15.	Pepperbox
7.	Flask	16.	Brush
8.	Iron	17.	Flask
9.	Brush		

Answer 37

For the outer wheels to go twice as fast as the inner wheels, the outer circle must have twice the circumference of the inner circle. Therefore the five feet between inner and outer wheels must be half the radius of the outer circle, giving the outer circle a diameter of 20 feet and a circumference of *pi* times 20, or 62.832 feet.

Answer 38

Pocahontas is 24 years old, little Captain John is 3.

Answer 39

The customer bought the 13- and 15-gallon barrels of oil at 50 cents per gallon, and the 8-, 17-, and 31-gallon barrels of vinegar at 25 cents per gallon. This left the 19-gallon barrel which may contain either oil or vinegar.

Answer 40

Each mark-down is 2/5 the former price, so the next price will be 51 cents and 2 mills.

Answer 41

The top illustration below shows the lines of march for the five guards, and the bottom illustration shows how the warder reached the dark cell by making only 16 turns.

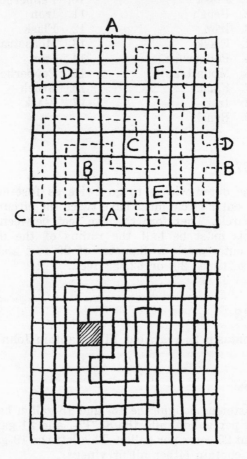

Answer 42

The five boys are counted out by using the number fourteen instead of thirteen. The count begins as before on the hatless girl at the top of the picture and moves clockwise around the circle.

Answer 43

Answer 44

[Let x stand for the cost of the hat Reuben actually bought and y for the cost of his suit. The hat Cynthia bought also has a value of y, and her dress will be $x-1$. We know that x plus y is $15. So if the $15 which they spent for hats is divided into two prices, one of which is 1 and 1/2 times the other, then the new prices must be $6 and $9. The data now permits the following equation:

$$9 + x - 1 = 6 + 15 - x$$

This shows x to be $6.50, the price Reuben paid for his hat. It follows that he paid $8.50 for his suit, and that she paid $8.50 for her hat and $5.50 for her dress. Total: $29.—M.G.]

Answer 45

Miss Bo-Peep must have had eight sheep in her flock. Eight posts arranged in a square will have the same area as ten posts in an oblong with five posts on the long side and two on the short.

Answer 46

Fido is ten years old and the sister is thirty.

Answer 47

A good rule to remember for false scales of the type described is this: weigh an article on one side of the scale, then on the other; multiply the two results together, and the square root of the result will be the true weight of the article.

Knowing that a pyramid weighs one ounce, the inspector's first weighing showed a cube to weigh 3/8 of an ounce. His second weighing, with the cube on the other pan, showed a cube to weigh six ounces. Six times 3/8 is 18/8 or 9/4, the square root of which is 3/2 or 1 and 1/2 ounces. Therefore a cube weighs 1 and 1/2 ounces, and on an honest scale eight cubes would balance with twelve pyramids.

Answer 48

The diagram below shows how the sixteen checkers are placed. The fact that two men must occupy squares at the center rules out many answers that otherwise would be as correct as the one shown here.

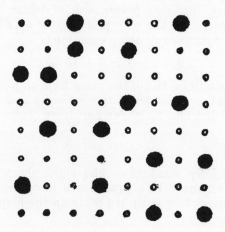

Answer 49

The popular answer to problems of this kind is to halve the total time to obtain an average speed, assuming that the wind boosts the rider's speed in one direction just as much as it retards it in the other direction. This is incorrect, because the wind has helped the rider for only three minutes, and hindered him for four minutes. If he could ride a mile in three minutes with the wind, he could go 1 and 1/3 miles in four minutes. He returns against the wind in the same four minutes, so he could go 2 and 1/3 miles in eight minutes, with the wind helping him half the time and hindering him half the time. The wind can therefore be ignored and we conclude that without the wind he could go 2 and 1/3 miles in eight minutes, or one mile in 3 and 3/7 minutes.

Answer 50

The number of children on the carousel, including Sammy himself, was thirteen.

Answer 51

One straight cut down through the center of the star and connecting the extreme points of the crescent will do the trick. Simply move the dark piece A (in the picture below) to the right as shown.

Answer 52

Last year Mrs. Wiggs raised 11,025 cabbages on a square with 105 patches on the side. This year she will raise 11,236 cabbages on a square with 106 patches on the side.

Answer 53

[In the answer section of the *Cyclopedia,* Loyd gives only solutions that are not legitimate ones. For example:

$$\begin{array}{r} 70 \\ 13 \\ 6 \\ 5 \\ 4 \\ \hline 98 \\ 2 \\ \hline 100 \end{array}$$

This requires two additions and clearly violates the conditions as stated.

Loyd also gives six answers using fractions (evidently the two dots could be used in place of the fraction line). For example:

$$\begin{array}{r} 24 \text{ and } 3/6 \\ 75 \text{ and } 9/18 \\ \hline 100 \end{array}$$

I do not know what Loyd had in mind for what he calls the "real answer" to his problem, but if we permit the four dots to be used as symbols for repeating decimals, in the manner of Loyd's "Columbus Problem" to be found elsewhere in this volume, it can be solved as follows:

$$\begin{array}{r} 79.\dot{3} \text{ (or 79 and 1/3)} \\ 8.\dot{6} \text{ (or 8 and 2/3)} \\ 5 \\ 4 \\ 2 \\ 1 \\ 0 \\ \hline 100 \end{array}$$

—M.G.]

Answer 54

We learn from the manner in which the nuts were divided that the girls' ages are in the proportions 9 : 12 : 14. Therefore the 700 chestnuts were divided so that the youngest girl got 198, the next oldest got 264, and the oldest got 308. As for the ages of the girls, they cannot be determined exactly. All we know is that their ages are in the proportions 9 : 12 : 14. Judging by the picture, a good guess would be 4-1/2, 6, and 7 years.

Answer 55

All puzzlists should know that the height of a tower or pole can be gauged by measuring the length of its shadow. A good illustration of the principle is found in Arthur Conan Doyle's novel, *The White Company*, when Sir Nigel and his gallant comrades are locked up in a besieged castle:

> The grizzled archer took several lengths of rope from his comrades and knotting them together he stretched them out in the long shadow, which the rising sun threw from the frowning keep. Then he fixed the yew-stave of his bow upon end and measured the long, thin, black line which it threw upon the turf. "A six-foot stave throws a twelve-foot shadow," he muttered. "The keep throws a shadow of sixty paces, so thirty paces of rope will be enough."

Here we have the secret of our puzzle. All shadows in the picture are in the same proportion to the height of the objects which cast them. A plumb line from the fingertip of the man who is pointing at the boy will show that the shadows are one third the heights of their objects. The pole therefore is three times the length of its shadow from the center of the pole's base to the end of the shadow line. By measuring the width of the trolley tracks at the spot where the pole's shadow falls, and remembering that the tracks are four feet and eight inches wide, we can guess the height of the pole to be not far from nineteen feet and eight inches.

Answer 56

[This confusing little problem can be attacked in a number of different ways. One way is to let *t* stand for the speed of the train, *c* for the speed of the coach, *x* for the distance from meeting point to Glasgow, and 189—x for the distance from Inverness to meeting point. The time it takes the coach to go from Inverness to the meeting spot can be equated with 189—$2x$ (the difference in miles between the two distances). This in turn can be equated with the time it takes the train to go from Glasgow to the meeting point. From these two equations we learn that the speed of the coach is one mile per hour greater than the speed of the train.

This information, together with the fact that the coach travels 189 miles in 12 hours less time than the train, enables us to set up an equation that proves the speed of the coach to be 4-1/2 miles per hour. The train's speed, therefore, is 3-1/2 miles per hour. It is now a simple matter to discover that the distance from the meeting spot to Glasgow is exactly 82 and 11/16 miles.—M.G.]

Answer 57

The second player can always win the daisy game by playing so as to divide the petals into two equal groups. For example, if the first player takes one petal, the second player takes two opposite petals to leave two groups of five each; and if the first player takes two petals, the second player takes one opposite petal to accomplish the same result. Thereafter, he simply imitates the plays of the first player. If the first player takes two petals to leave a 2-1 combination in one group, the second player takes the corresponding two petals to leave a 2-1 combination in the other group. In this way he is sure to get the last play.

Answer 58

The 3/4-pound weight is clearly equal to 1/4 of a brick; therefore, a brick must weigh 12/4 or 3 pounds.

Answer 59

Four ships move to the center as shown below to make four rows, each row with four ships. The fifth row is the horizontal row at the bottom.

Answer 60

Each oval piece is cut into three parts as shown in Figure 4; then the six pieces are fitted together to make the circular table top shown in Figure 3.

[See Henry Dudeney's *Amusements in Mathematics*, "Problem No. 157," for another six-piece solution to this old puzzle. Sam Loyd later discovered a four-piece solution in which the holes are transverse instead of lengthwise, and which may be found in Dudeney's *Puzzles and Curious Problems*, "Problem No. 183."—M.G.]

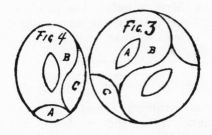

Answer 61

It will be found that there are 372 ways of spelling "Red Rum," all ending at the center of the square. Then comes the curious feature of the puzzle (although it is self-evident) that there must be just as many ways of spelling "Murder" as there are of spelling "Red Rum." Therefore, the square of 372, which is 138,384, gives us the total number of different ways to spell "Red Rum & Murder."

Answer 62

[Loyd's solution to his first Monad puzzle is shown in the center picture below. The end pictures show the solution to his third puzzle. He answers the second puzzle by saying no more than to make a straight cut from A to B in the middle picture. For the precise location of points A and B, together with a pretty proof that it does in fact divide the Yin and Yang into two pieces of equal area, consult Henry Dudeney's *Amusements in Mathematics*, "Problem 158." See also his "Problem 160" for a slightly different version of Loyd's third problem.—M.G.]

Answer 63

[Formulating the equations for this problem is more difficult than one might suspect. If x is the distance from the hotel to the wayhouse, then the man walks $x-4$ miles while the coach is waiting thirty minutes. The man's rate, therefore, is $2x-8$ miles per hour. Because the man walks 4 miles while the coach goes x miles, we can express the coach's rate at

$$\frac{x(x-4)}{2}.$$

Two equations involving x and y can now be written, y being the distance from the wayhouse to Piketown. One equates the time it takes the man to walk the entire distance minus one mile with the time it takes the coach to go the entire distance plus 30 minutes. The other equates the time it takes the man to walk from the wayhouse to Piketown plus 15 minutes with the time it takes the coach to make the same trip plus 30 minutes. The equations give x a value of 6, y a value of 3, making a total distance from hotel to Piketown of 9 miles. The coach travels at 6 miles per hour, the man at 4.—M.G.]

Answer 64

Two pitchers balance with three plates, so we know that one plate is equal to 2/3 of a pitcher. Now let us add a glass to each side of the scales in the second illustration to make the left arm the same as the left arm in the first illustration.

This proves that the pitcher is equal to a plate and two glasses; and since the plate equals 2/3 of a pitcher, the two glasses must make up the other 1/3. Each glass, therefore, is 1/6 of a pitcher.

In the first illustration we see that a glass (1/6 of a pitcher) and a bottle balance with a pitcher, which tells us that a bottle must be 5/6 of a pitcher. Therefore, to balance the bottle in the bottom picture we will need five glasses.

Answer 65

The additional stock of liquor bought by the agent increased his stock to $343 wholesale. On this he put an advance of 10 per cent, giving it a retail price of $377.30. He sold $285.80 at retail, which leaves $91.50 on hand as shown in the picture. This stock would be worth $83.18 wholesale. Subtracting this from $343 (the wholesale value of the entire stock) shows that $259.82 wholesale worth of liquor was sold. We subtract this from the total retail sales of $285.80 to find that the town's profit on liquor sales was $25.98.

This can be checked as follows: The profit of $25.98 added to the $12 cash advanced at the outset and the $59.50 worth of liquor totals $97.48. From this we subtract the agent's commission of $14.29 to leave $83.19 for the wholesale worth of the liquor which remains, showing the agent's accounts to be correct within two cents.

Answer 66

The charitable lady had 42 cents when she started her walk.

Answer 67

The two children were so befogged over the calendar that they had started on their way to school on Sunday morning!

Answer 68

[Let x represent the total number of poles and y the number of hours it takes the car to go 3 and 5/8 miles. The car will pass x poles in y hours, x/y poles in one hour, and $x/60y$ poles in one minute. Since we are told that 3 and 5/8 times the number of poles in one minute equals the car's speed in miles per hour, we can write the following equation:

$$\frac{3\frac{5}{8}x}{60y} = \frac{3\frac{5}{8}}{y}$$

In solving the equation, we note that the car's speed of 3 and 5/8 over y cancels out of both sides, giving us 60 as the value of x. In other words, the data hold regardless of how fast or slow the car goes, which is the most bewildering feature of the problem.

We know that 60 is the total number of poles in 3 and 5/8 miles or 19,140 feet, but since there are 59 spaces between 60 poles, we divide 19,140 by 59 to obtain 324 and 24/59 feet as the distance between two poles.—M.G.]

Answer 69

Five odd "figures" will add to 14 as follows:

$$\begin{array}{r} 11 \\ 1 \\ 1 \\ 1 \\ \hline 14 \end{array}$$

Answer 70

The following diagram shows the answer to this remarkably difficult puzzle.

Answer 71

The checkerboard can be divided into eighteen different pieces as shown:

[There are many different ways that the board can be divided into eighteen different pieces. As an interesting exercise, the reader may try to work out a proof that eighteen is indeed the maximum number.—M.G.]

Answer 72

The kettle, like a bucket or lamp shade, is in the shape of a frustum of a cone, which is simply a cone with its top cut off parallel to the base. Its volume can be found by subtracting the cut-off cone from the larger cone, or more simply by the formula:

$$\frac{\pi h}{3}(R^2 + r^2 + Rr)$$

In this formula h stands for the height of the frustum, and the upper- and lower-case R's for the radii of its top and bottom. In regard to the kettle, we know the height to be 12 inches, and one radius to be twice the other. If we let R stand for the base radius and $2R$ for the top radius, the volume will prove to be pi times $28R^2$. Because the volume is 25 gallons or 5,775 cubic inches, it is easy to compute the brim's diameter at a little more than 32 inches.

Answer 73

Each week the charitable lady distributed $120 to her pensioners. The original number of men was 20.

Answer 74

One way to form the eight desired fractions is as follows (some of the numbers can be varied slightly and yet give the same fraction):

$$\frac{6729}{13458} = \frac{1}{2}, \qquad \frac{5832}{17496} = \frac{1}{3}, \qquad \frac{4392}{17568} = \frac{1}{4},$$

$$\frac{2769}{13845} = \frac{1}{5}, \qquad \frac{2943}{17658} = \frac{1}{6}, \qquad \frac{2394}{16758} = \frac{1}{7},$$

$$\frac{3187}{25496} = \frac{1}{8}, \qquad \frac{6381}{57429} = \frac{1}{9}.$$

Answer 75

The couplet concealed on the beehive is:

How doth the little busy bee
Improve each shining hour?

Answer 76

Each lad started with $25. Jim bet $15 at 15 to 1 odds and won $225, giving him a capital of $250. Jack bet $10 at 10 to 1 odds and won $100, giving him a capital of $125, or just half as much as Jim.

Answer 77

There were 14 horses and 22 riders in the circus. We know that the zoo contained 56 feet and 20 heads. We can see ten animals and seven birds in the picture, which accounts for 17 heads and 54 feet, leaving 3 heads and 2 feet unaccounted for. It does not require a vivid imagination to surmise that the attraction in the case which excites so much attention must be a Hindu snake-charmer with two serpents.

Answer 78

Farmer Jones started with 719 melons. He sold 576 for a dollar per dozen ($48), and the remaining 143 at a price of thirteen for a dollar ($11), bringing him a total of $59 for all 719 melons.

[A triangular pyramid of 120 melons can be combined with one of 560 melons to make a larger triangular pyramid of 680 melons. The formula for these tetrahedral numbers is:

$$\frac{1}{6n} (n+1)(n+2)$$

—M.G.]

Answer 79

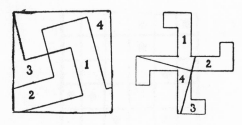

Answer 80

Answer 81

Since we are not told the length of the rails, we have no way of knowing how many acres each field contains. It is not necessary, however, to know this to solve the problem. The areas of the two fields are in the proportion of 209 to 210; therefore, the farmers lose 1/210th of the area of their old lot. They lose squashes in the same proportion. Since 1/210th of 840 squashes in 4 squashes, we conclude that they lose 4 squashes for every acre on their old lot.

Answer 82

The four rings weigh a quarter of a pound, three quarters of a pound, two and one quarter pounds, and six and three quarters pounds. By clever juggling with the weights, placing them if need be on both sides of the scale, any weight from one quarter to ten pounds can be weighed to the nearest quarter-pound.

Answer 83

One watch gets three minutes ahead of the other every hour, so after twenty hours it would be one hour ahead.

Answer 84

A dozen eggs can be placed in the crate as shown.

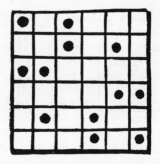

Answer 85

The problem is readily solved by working backward. I started with $260, the baron had $80, and the count $140.

Answer 86

The boy is five years old.

Answer 87

There were fifteen bees.

Answer 88

The common stock was worth $6,000,000.

Answer 89

Altogether there are 12 cuffs and 18 collars. Collars cost 2 cents each and cuffs 2-1/2 cents, so the cost of Charlie's bundle will be 39 cents.

Answer 90

In that interesting problem of the reapers who cut a swath around a rectangular field until half the crop was gathered, I find that they had a simple rule. They said: "One quarter the difference between a short cut cross lots, and round by the road." Mathematicians will understand it better if we say: from the sum of the two sides subtract the diagonal of the field and divide the remainder by four.

The field was 2,000 yards long by 1,000 yards wide. Using a tape line, those honest farmers found that the diagonal from one corner to the opposite one was a little over 2,236 yards. To go "round by the road," of course, was 3,000 yards, so the difference was a little less than 764 yards. One quarter of this is just a bit shy of 191 yards (190.983), which is the width the border strip should be.

Answer 91

The grandfather clock stopped at exactly 49 minutes, 5 and 5/11 seconds past nine o'clock.

Answer 92

Six arrows will score 100 by registering 17, 17, 17, 17, 16, 16.

Answer 93

(1) Figure 1 shows how a square can be cut into five pieces to make two Greek crosses of the same size. One piece is in the form of a cross, and the other four pieces will make the second one. After this puzzle became well known, I found

a way to achieve the same result by cutting the square into only four pieces as shown in Figure 2. These pieces will then form the two crosses on the right.

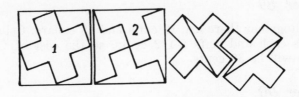

(2) To cut a square into five pieces that will make two Greek crosses of different sizes, cut the square as shown in the drawing on the left. Piece A is a small cross, and the other four pieces will form a larger cross as shown on the right.

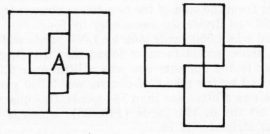

(3) The illustration below shows how a Greek cross can be cut into five pieces to make two crosses of equal size. One cross is formed of one piece. The remaining pieces fit together to make the second one.

[For a full discussion of Greek-cross dissection puzzles, see the section on them in Henry Dudeney's *Amusements in Mathematics.*—M.G.]

Answer 94

There is a pretty way of solving this problem without having to stumble over square roots. We first divide 600 by 250, then add 2 to obtain 4.4. Six hundred divided by 4.4 will give us the distance from the boy on the right to the bridge on the left, a distance of 136 and 4/11 yards. This added to 250 (the same boy's distance from the bridge on the right) gives 386 and 4/11 as the distance between the bridges, and the answer to the problem.

[The puzzling thing about this short-cut formula, which applies to all right triangles, is that added constant of 2. Suppose we let a stand for the distance from the boy on the right to the left bridge, b for his distance from the right bridge, c for the 600-yard side of the triangle, and d for the hypotenuse. The Pythagorean theorem tells us that the square of the sum of a and b plus the square of c equals the square of d. We also know that a plus d equals b plus c, or d equals b plus c minus a. Substituting this value for d in the previous equation we find that, in reducing the equation, all the squared terms cancel out. We are left with the formula

$$\frac{bc}{2b+c} \quad \text{which can be written} \quad \frac{c}{\dfrac{c}{b}+2}.$$

—M.G.]

Answer 95

Each Grace had 144 apples at the start, and each Muse had 48 flowers, 12 of each color. Each Grace gave a dozen apples to each Muse, and each Muse gave four flowers (one of each color) to each Grace. After the exchange, every girl will have 36 apples and 36 flowers (nine of each color).

Answer 96

The boy with the number 6 stood on his head so that the three of them could form the number 931.

Answer 97

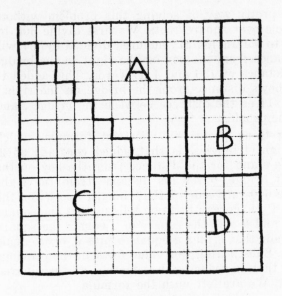

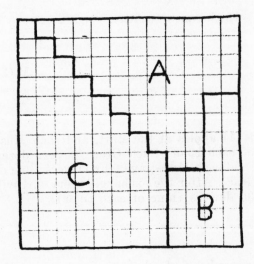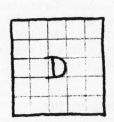

Answer 98

In the matter of dividing the O'Shaugnessy estate, it is clear that it was designed to give the mother twice as much as the daughter, and the son twice as much as the mother. It is a simple matter to carry out the terms of the bequest by giving the daughter one seventh, the mother two sevenths, and the son four sevenths.

Answer 99

The rancher had seven sons and fifty-six cows. The eldest son took two cows, and his wife took six. The next son took three cows and his wife five. The next son took four and his wife four, and so on down to the seventh son who took eight cows, leaving none for his wife. Curiously, each family now has eight cows, so·each took one of the seven horses to make their livestock of equal value.

Answer 100

The nine digits add up to 45 which is a multiple of nine. Regardless of how these digits and zero are arranged to make two numbers, the sum of the two numbers will also be a multiple of nine.

Moreover, when you add the digits in any multiple of nine, the result is always a multiple of nine. So we have only to add the digits we see in the answer to obtain 10, then subtract this from 18 (the nearest multiple of nine that is greater than 10) to obtain 8, the missing digit.

Answer 101

The horse trotted the four quarters of the mile in 27-1/4, 27, 27-1/8, and 27-1/8 minutes, respectively, making the total time 1 minute and 48-1/2 seconds.

Answer 102

To put the elephant in the center of the Siamese flag, cut it into two pieces as shown, then turn around the diamond-shaped piece.

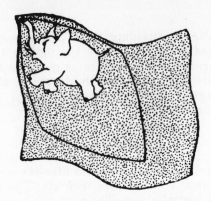

The shortest route on the plan of the orchard is: 15, 16, 12, 11, 10, 14, 13, 9, 5, 1, 2, 6, 7, 8, 4, 3, heart.

Answer 103

[Let x be the number of acres and y the number of bushels. We can write these two equations:

$$\frac{\frac{3}{4}y + 80}{x} = 7$$

$$\frac{y + 80}{x} = 8$$

Solving the equations shows the number of bushels to be 80 and the farm to contain 20 acres.—M.G.]

Answer 104

[If x is the number of pounds of turkey Mrs. O'Flaherty bought, as well as the number of pounds of geese, then we can write this equation:

$$\frac{21x}{24} + \frac{21x}{18} = 2x + 2$$

The equation gives x a value of 48. Therefore, Mrs. O'Flaherty spent $11.52 for turkey and $8.64 for geese, or $20.16 altogether.—M.G.]

Answer 105

The suit sold for $13.75.

Answer 106

Jimmy is 10 and 16/21 years old.

Answer 107

[Loyd's *Cyclopedia* does not explain the strategy of winning this game, but it is the same as the game of "Puss in the Corner," to be found in Henry Dudeney's *Amusements in Mathematics*, "Problem 394." The farmer's strategy is to play to diagonally opposite corners of squares until he forces the turkey to the border, after which he wins easily. If the farmer plays first, he must move to cell 35. There is no way the turkey can seize the advantage because the spot between 9 and 10 is blank. The following typical game should make the strategy clear:

Turkey	Farmer
8	50
30	47
29	46
37	45
29	38
28	37
51	29
60	51 (wins) —M.G.]

The second puzzle is solved in twenty-four moves as follows: 52, 14, 15, 8, 9, 16, 18, 10, 11, 42, 39, 31, 33, 25, 22, 45, 50, 4, 5, 64, 60, 2, 3, 7.

Answer 108

As the picture below indicates, the jeweler stole a gem from each end of the horizontal row, then simply moved the bottom diamond to the top.

Answer 109

[This is simply a variation of "The Remnant Puzzle" which appears in this volume as Puzzle 80. By placing the triangle against the square as shown in the first figure of the solution to "The Remnant Puzzle," the problem can be solved in five pieces. Because the triangle in this puzzle is smaller in proportion to the square than the triangle in the previous puzzle, the other two methods of placing the triangle are not applicable.—M.G.]

Answer 110

Mrs. O'Neill spent $33.60 on bananas. This would buy 48 bunches each of red and yellow bananas, or 96 in all. But by dividing the amount in half and spending $16.80 for red bunches and $16.80 for yellow, she could buy 42 bunches of the red and 56 bunches of the yellow, or 98 in all.

Answer 111

Jocko took the windows in the order: 10, 11, 12, 8, 4, 3, 7, 6, 2, 1, 5, 9. This route travels the wide space between the bottom and middle rows of windows only twice.

Answer 112

The puzzle can be solved in eight moves as follows: Taft jumps Knox, Johnson, La Follette, and Cannon in succession. Gray jumps Fairbanks. Hughes jumps Bryan. Gray jumps Hughes. Taft jumps Gray.

[If we regard a series of connected jumps by one man as a single move, then Loyd's solution requires five moves. It can be done, however, in as few as four moves. The four-move solution will be found in Henry Dudeney's *Amusements in Mathematics,* "Problem No. 229."—M.G.]

Answer 113

Answer 114

The die must have shown a 1 on top. This added to 4 on the side gives a score of 5 for one player. The remaining side numbers—4, 2, and 3—add to 10 for the other player, who wins by 5 points.

The sextimal notation for 109,778 is 2,204,122. The digit on the right end represents units, the next digit gives the number of 6's, the third digit represents 36's, the fourth digit represents 216's, and so on. The system is based on the powers of 6 instead of the powers of 10 as in our decimal notation.

Answer 115

The carpenter's problem can be solved in three pieces as shown.

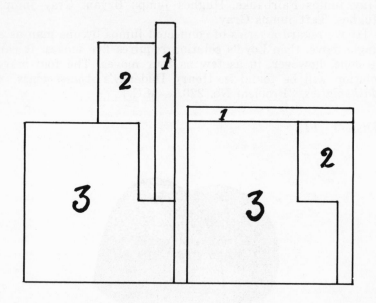

Answer 116

The children bought three pieces of fudge, fifteen chocolate drops, and two gum drops.

Answer 117

It would seem at first blush as if any number of fish from 33 to 43 might have been caught, because A could receive from zero to 11 fish and the quantities received by the others become apparent. However, since each boy finally received the same number of fish, it is clear that the total number must be 35 or 40. If we try the latter figure, we find that it meets all the conditions. A caught 8 fish, B caught 6, C, 14, D, 4, and E, 8. After B, C, and D pool their catch and divide it into thirds, each boy will have 8 fish. No matter how they join and divide their stocks, the share of each will remain 8.

Answer 118

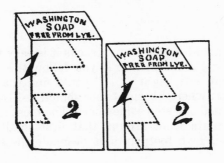

Answer 119

The boardinghouse pie can be cut into 22 pieces, as shown. The letters "TM" show how Aunt Mary marked her pies so as to tell whether 'tis mince or 'taint mince:

[This classic problem takes on added interest if one seeks the formula by which one can calculate the maximum number of pieces for any given number of cuts. For two related problems, involving the cutting of a crescent and a cylindrical piece of cheese, see Volume One of *Mathematical Puzzles of Sam Loyd.*—M.G.]

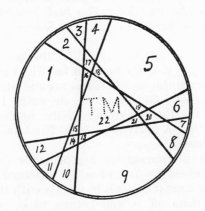

Answer 120

Susie paid five cents for silk, four cents for worsted.

Answer 121

At the start of Santa Claus' tracks it is easy to distinguish the left from right footprints. If you follow the tracks, counting "left, right, left, right . . . ," you'll find that Santa's left foot is at a spot where his right foot should be! In other words, Santa has gained one step somewhere. The most likely explanation is that Santa went around that first small circle *twice,* stepping on his own footprints as he made the second round.

Answer 122

Tell scored 100 by shooting 11 twice and 13 six times. The shadow of the net stake near Tell's left foot is half the height of the stake. The shadow of the flagpole is 35 yards, so we estimate the height of the pole at 70 yards or 210 feet.

Answer 123

[Loyd's *Cyclopedia* does not answer this difficult problem. (A purported answer proves to be the answer to an altogether different tandem bicycle problem that does not appear in the *Cyclopedia,* but may be found on page 65 of another collection, *Sam Loyd and His Puzzles.*) The best procedure, supported by the answers to similar problems in Dudeney's puzzle books, seems to be as follows:

C, the slowest walker, always rides the tandem. He and A, the fastest walker, ride the tandem for 31.04 miles while B is walking. A dismounts, and C turns around and rides back to pick up B at a spot 5.63 miles from the start. B and C remain on the bicycle for the remainder of the journey, arriving at the same time that A arrives on foot. The total time is a little less than 2.3 hours.

The problem is approached algebraically by letting x be the distance walked by B and y the distance walked by A. By equating the time it takes B to walk x with the time it takes the bicycle to drop off A and return to B, one equation is obtained. A second equation is obtained by equating the time it takes A to walk y with the time it takes the bicycle to complete the journey after dropping off A. The two simultaneous equations are solved for x and y, and the rest follows.—M.G.]

Answer 124

The third triangle has sides of 30 and 224, and a hypotenuse of 226. [There is no limit to the number of different right-triangles that can be found which are equal in area and which have integral sides. For a simple method of obtaining such triangles, consult Henry Dudeney's *The Canterbury Puzzles*, "Problem No. 107."—M.G.]

Answer 125

On Saturday Mrs. Bargainhunter bought ten plates at 13 cents each. She returned them Monday for 18 saucers at 3 cents each and eight cups at 12 cents each, making a total of $1.50 (she had returned the ten plates at 15 cents each). On Saturday her $1.30 would have purchased thirteen cups at 10 cents each.

Answer 126

The milkman started with 5-1/2 gallons of water in can A and 2-1/2 gallons of milk in can B. At the finish of his pouring operations, can A contained 3 gallons of water and 1 of milk and can B contained 2-1/2 gallons of water and 1-1/2 of milk.

[Loyd does not explain how he arrived at these figures, but the problem can be solved as follows. Let x be the original amount of liquid in can A and y the original amount in B. It is easy to discover algebraically that the proportion of x to y must be 11 to 5, but we still do not know if this is the proportion of water to milk or milk to water. Let's assume the latter and begin our pouring operations with 11 units of milk and 5 units of water. We will end with 3 units of water and 5 of milk in can B, but this contradicts the fact that B at the finish has one gallon more of water than milk.

We must conclude, therefore, that we begin with 11 units of water and 5 of milk. Our operations end with 3 units of milk and 5 of water in can B. Since the water exceeds the milk by one gallon, 5 units minus 3 units must equal one gallon, which makes our unit equal to 1/2 gallon. Eleven units of water will then be 5-1/2 gallons, and 5 units of milk will be 2-1/2 gallons.—M.G.]

Answer 127

The distance between stations is 200 miles.

[An algebraic solution is easily obtained by letting x be the distance traveled during the first hour and y be the remaining distance. The train's normal speed in miles per hour will be x, its crippled speed will be $3x/5$, and the normal time for the run will be $\dfrac{x+y}{x}$.

The data permit the following two equations:

$$1 + \frac{5y}{3x} = \frac{x+y}{x} + 2$$

$$\frac{x+50}{x} + \frac{5y-250}{3x} = \frac{x+y}{x} + 1\tfrac{1}{3}$$

These equations reduce to:

$$3x = y$$

$$2x = y - 50$$

Subtracting one equation from the other yields a value of 50 for x, 150 for y, making the total distance 200 miles.—M.G.]

Answer 128

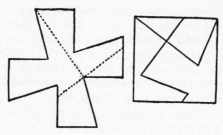

Answer 129

The names of the four girls are Ann Jones, May Robinson, Jane Smith, and Kate Brown.

Answer 130

Each boy had 100 marbles.

Answer 131

The Chinese merchant used 30 pounds of the five-bit tea and 10 pounds of the three-bit tea in his mixture.

Answer 132

The Boss is 84 years old.

Answer 133

Figure 1 shows how nine eggs can be placed to make ten rows, each with three eggs. Figure 2 shows how to mark off the nine eggs with four continuous strokes.

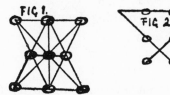

[The second problem, a classic geometrical puzzle, is often cited by psychologists as an example of how the mind tends to impose unnecessary limitations upon methods of attacking problems. Nothing whatever was said about confining the strokes to the area inside the square formation.—M.G.]

Answer 134

Arranging the twelve rails in the form of a regular dodecagon (12-sided polygon) provides the maximum area: a little more than 2,866 square feet.

Answer 135

The car traveled 71-3/8 miles the first hour, 63-5/8 miles the second hour, 55-7/8 the third, and 48-1/8 the fourth. The difference between each hour is 7-3/4 miles. [The problem can be solved by letting x stand for the mileage of the last hour, x plus y for the third hour, x plus $2y$ for the second, and x plus $3y$ for the first. We now have two linear equations: (1) $2x$ plus $5y$ equals 135; (2) $2x$ plus y equals 104.—M.G.]

Answer 136

$$
\begin{array}{l}
80.\dot{5}\ \ (\text{or } 55/99) \\
.\dot{9}\dot{7}\ \ (\text{or } 97/99) \\
.\dot{4}\dot{6}\ \ (\text{or } 46/99) \\
\hline
82.
\end{array}
$$

Answer 137

[Let $1/x$ be Maude's time to skate the mile. Jennie's time will then be $1/2.5x$, and we can write the following equation:

$$
\frac{1}{x} - \frac{1}{2.5} = 6
$$

This gives x a value .1, making Jennie's time 4 minutes and Maude's 10.—M.G.]

Answer 138

[This problem is not answered in Loyd's *Cyclopedia* but it is easily solved by algebra. Let x be the total number of miles traveled, y the time it takes to go, and z the time it takes to return. We know that x/y equals 5, x/z equals 3, and y plus z equals 7. From these equations we find that the round trip was 13-1/8 miles.—M.G.]

Answer 139

[After falling 20 feet, a body is traveling at a speed of 35.777 feet per second (the square of the velocity of a falling object is equal to twice the acceleration times the distance). A 30-pound object would therefore have a momentum at this speed of 1,073.310. The goats have a combined weight of 111 pounds, so in order to butt each other with a momentum equal to the skull-cracking momentum of 1,073.310, they must have an approach speed of at least 9.669 feet per second.—M.G.]

Answer 140

The watchman, his wife, baby, and dog escape as follows:

1. Lower baby.
2. Lower dog, raise baby.
3. Lower man, raise dog.
4. Lower baby.
5. Lower dog, raise baby.
6. Lower baby.
7. Lower wife, raise all others.
8. Lower baby.
9. Lower dog, raise baby.
10. Lower baby.
11. Lower man, raise dog.
12. Lower dog, raise baby.
13. Lower baby.

[This is a simplified version of a problem proposed by Lewis Carroll, and which may be found on page 318 of *The Lewis Carroll Picture Book,* edited by Stuart Dodgson Collingwood, 1899.—M.G.]

Answer 141

If the eagle traveled 500 miles per day, it would take it 39 days to go 19,500 miles. But in going around the earth it gains an extra day, so the correct answer is 38 days.

Answer 142

There are 31 different equilateral triangles in King Solomon's seal.

Answer 143

The diameter of the circular track has no bearing on the problem. When they meet, the hare has gone 1/6 of the way and the tortoise has gone 17/24. The tortoise has therefore been moving 17/4 times as fast as the hare. The hare has 5/6 of the distance yet to go as compared to 1/6 for the tortoise, so the hare must go five times faster than the tortoise, or 84/4 faster than he went before.

Answer 144

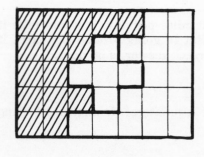
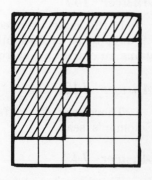

Answer 145

The diagram below shows how the board may be wired from B to A with 233 inches of wire.

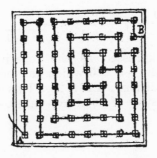

Answer 146

[Loyd gives the answers to both parts of this problem, but does not explain how to get them. Part I is most simply approached as follows:

Let 1 be the length of the army and the time it takes the army to march its length. The army's speed will also be 1. Let x be the total distance traveled by the courier and also his speed. On the courier's forward trip, his speed relative to the moving army will be $x-1$. On the return trip his speed relative to the army will be $x+1$. Each trip is a distance of 1 (relative to the army), and the two trips are completed in unit time, so we can write the following equation:

$$\frac{1}{x-1} + \frac{1}{x+1} = 1$$

This can be expressed as the quadratic: $x^2 - 2x - 1 = 0$, for which x has the positive value of $1 + \sqrt{2}$. We multiply this by 50 to get the final answer of 120.7+ miles. In other words, the courier travels a distance equal to the length of the army plus that same length times the square root of 2.

Part II can be approached in the same manner. In this version the courier's speed relative to the moving army is $x-1$ on his forward trip, $x+1$ on his backward trip, and $\sqrt{x^2-1}$ on his two diagonal trips. (It does not matter where he starts his round trip, so to simplify the problem we think of him as starting at a rear corner of the square instead of at the center of the rear.) As before, each trip is a distance of 1 relative to the army, and since he completes the four trips in unit time we can write:

$$\frac{1}{x-1} + \frac{1}{x+1} + \frac{2}{\sqrt{x^2-1}} = 1$$

This can be expressed as the fourth degree equation: $x^4 - 4x^3 - 2x^2 + 4x + 5 = 0$ which has only one root that fits the problem's conditions: 4.18112+. This is multiplied by 50 to get the final answer of 209.056+ miles.—M.G.]

Answer 147

Answer 148

Knowing that each shelf contains just twenty quarts, let us begin by cancelling off six little jars from each of the two lower shelves. We are left with two big jars on the middle shelf and four medium ones on the lower shelf, which proves that one big jar holds as much jam as two medium ones.

Replace the cancelled jars, then cancel the two large ones on the middle shelf and their equivalent on the top shelf: one large jar and two medium ones. This leaves one medium and three small jars on the top shelf and six small jars on the middle shelf, proving that a medium jar holds as much as three little ones.

Now replace all the large jars with two medium ones; then replace all the medium ones with three small ones. This gives us 54 small jars altogether. If 54 small jars hold 60 quarts, then one small jar will hold 1-1/9 quarts, a medium jar will hold 3-1/3 quarts, and a large jar, 6-2/3 quarts.

Answer 149

The shortest path for the wire is one which runs along the floor, the two ends of the room, and one side wall. If we imagine the room to be a cardboard box that can be cut and folded flat as shown in the illustration below, the shortest path will be the hypotenuse of a right-angle triangle with sides of 39 and 15 feet. The length of this path is a trifle more than 41.78 feet.

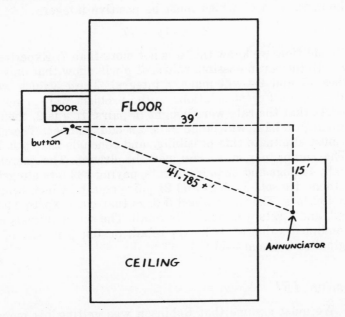

[This is Loyd's version of Henry Dudeney's famous "Spider and the Fly" problem, to be found in Dudeney's *The Canterbury Puzzles*. By altering the dimensions of the room, Loyd changed the problem so that it calls for a different method of cutting and folding flat the room.—M.G.]

Answer 150

[Although Loyd gives this puzzle a minor spot in his *Cyclopedia,* and answers it without explaining the solution, it is one of the most interesting problems in the book, combining algebraic with Diophantine analysis.

One way to tackle it is to let x be the number of dogs originally purchased and also the number of rats. The number of dogs among the seven animals left will be represented by y, and the number of rats left will be $7-y$. The number of dogs sold (at 2.2 bits each, which is an advance of ten per cent over cost) will then be $x-y$, and the number of rats sold (at 2.2 bits per pair or 1.1 bits each) will be $x-7-y$.

Expressing the data in the form of equations and simplifying them leads to the following Diophantine equation with two unknowns, both of which must be positive integers:

$$3x = 11y + 77$$

In addition, we know that y is not more than 7. Experimenting with the seven possible values of y will show that only two values—5 and 2—will make x integral. These values would lead to two different solutions to the problem were it not for the fact that the rats were bought in pairs. If y is 2, then the original purchase will be 33 rats, an odd number. Therefore we must eliminate this possibility and conclude that y is 5.

The complete picture can now be drawn. The merchant bought 44 dogs and 22 pairs of rats, paying 132 bits altogether for them. He sold 39 dogs and 21 pairs of rats, which brought him 132 bits. There remained 5 dogs that were worth 11 bits retail, and 2 rats worth 2.2 bits retail. The seven animals have a combined value of 13.2 bits retail, or ten per cent of his original investment.—M.G.]

Answer 151

We must assume that Robinson was getting his money's worth when he paid $2,500 for a third interest in the firm of Brown and Jones. Therefore the firm stock was worth $7,500 before Robinson entered. Brown, owning one and one half as much interest as Jones, possessed a $4,500 interest, and Jones, $3,000. Robinson's $2,500 was to be divided so that each of the three partners should have an equal interest, or $2,500 invested. Therefore Brown received $2,000 of Robinson's purchase money and Jones received $500.

Answer 152

Mrs. Hogan's piece of clothes line was 58⅓ feet, and Mary O'Neill's piece was 41⅔ feet.

Answer 153

One cow cost $150 and the other cost $50.

Answer 154

[Loyd's steeplechase puzzle is a variation of a problem to be found in most introductory calculus textbooks. (It is usually presented in terms of a man in a rowboat who wishes to reach a point on the shore ahead of him by rowing to the shore at a certain speed, then walking along the shore at a faster rate.)

The problem is solved by letting x be the distance from the far corner of the road to the spot where the horses leap the wall, and $1-x$ be the distance from this spot to the one-mile marker. We know that a horse has a speed of 35 miles per hour along the road and 26¼ miles per hour on the rough ground. The total time for reaching the goal via the shortcut will then be:

$$\frac{\sqrt{x^2 + 9/16}}{26\frac{1}{4}} + \frac{1 - x}{35}$$

The question is: what value for the independent variable x will minimize the above expression? We find the derivative of the equation, equate to zero, and solve for x. The value of x proves to be about .85 miles, which means that the best spot to jump the wall is about .15 or a little more than 1/7 of a mile beyond the one-mile sign.—M.G.]

Answer 155

The ten coins can be arranged as follows to produce 18 even rows:

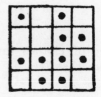

Answer 156

[If we let x be Mrs. Smith's money and y be Mr. Smith's, then the price of the grove and stream will equal $y/3$ and also equal $x/4$. In addition, we know that $3x/4$ plus y equals \$5,000, and $2y/3$ plus x equals \$5,000. From these equations we find that his money is \$2,500, her's is \$3,333 and $\frac{1}{3}$, and the cost of grove and stream is \$833 and $\frac{1}{3}$.—M.G.]

Answer 157

Whittington's cat catches all the mice by taking the route: A-4-C-1-Y-5-2-B-6-X-3-Z. If it takes six seconds for the clock to strike six, then each interval between strikes will be 1-1/5 seconds. In striking eleven there are ten such intervals, so the total time would be 12 seconds.

Answer 158

[Let x be the cost of keep. We can now write the following equation: $x - 34 = 13 + \frac{1}{4}x$, which gives x a value of $62\frac{2}{3}$. We subtract from this the \$34 profit to obtain a total loss of $28\frac{2}{3}$ dollars.—M.G.]

Answer 159

This is how Bo-Peep arranged the eight bars to form three squares of the same size:

Answer 160

The land was divided into 18 lots.

Answer 161

Move B and C to the right end of the line, next to the drummer girl. Fill gap with E and F. Fill gap with H and B. Fill gap with A and E.

Answer 162

Bill Jones got $8,836, his wife Mary got $5,476, and their son, Ned, $2,116. Hank Smith received $16,129, his wife Elizabeth got $12,769, and their daughter, Susan, $9,409. Jake Brown got $6,724, his wife Sarah, $3,364, and their son, Tom, the black sheep of the flock, only $4.

[Each number is, of course, a perfect square—a condition imposed by the manner in which the money was placed in the envelopes.—M.G.]

Answer 163

There were three boys and three girls. Each received one of the two-for-a-penny buns and two three-for-a-penny buns.

Answer 164

Bill Sykes worked 16⅔ days and loafed 13⅓ days.

Answer 165

[There is no answer to this puzzle in Loyd's *Cyclopedia*. Placing unlettered counters on the diagram is not difficult. If we imagine the spots to be wooden disks connected by string, we can open out the string into one large circle on which the disks will be strung in the following order: 1-3-5-7-9-11-13-2-4-6-8-10-12. It is now easy to see the strategy that must be followed if we wish to place all twelve counters on the spots. Suppose we put the first counter on No. 13. The next counter must be placed on either 4 or 9, then slid to either 11 or 2 where it will be adjacent to 13 in the series given above. The third counter must now be placed so that it can be slid to a spot adjacent to either end of the counters already placed, and so on for the remaining counters.

I do not know what word Loyd had in mind for the second half of his puzzle, but I suspect that it was "Wooloomooloo," the name of a bay in Port Jackson, the harbor on which Sydney, Australia is situated. The name is now spelled with thirteen letters—Woolloomooloo—but apparently the twelve-letter spelling was correct in Loyd's day for he gives this form of the word as the answer to a puzzle called "The Kangaroo Puzzle" which appears elsewhere in his *Cyclopedia*.

The "Kangaroo Puzzle" was designed to illustrate the fact, Loyd tells us, that every word has a "mechanical peculiarity of its own, susceptible of being illustrated in puzzle form." The puzzle makes use of the following diagram:

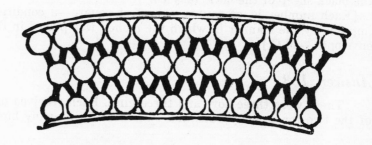

The problem is to place a twelve-letter word on the top row of circles, the letters in proper order, then move them down to the bottom row. This is done either by moving each letter one step at a time along the black lines, or by jumping one letter over another as in checkers. At the finish, the letters must spell the same word correctly on the bottom row. Any twelve-letter word will work, but the task is to find a word that will work in the fewest number of moves, counting a jump as a single move. "Wooloomooloo" solves the puzzle in twenty moves.

In Loyd's time Woolloomooloo was the bay where all American liners docked at Sydney, and apparently a familiar name to most of his readers. It is hard to imagine that there could be another English word capable of solving his "Henry George Puzzle."—M.G.]

Answer 166

If we let x be the bridge's length in feet, then the cow stands $\frac{1}{2}x - 2$ from one end and $\frac{1}{2}x + 5$ from the other. The train is $2x$ from the nearest end.

The cow can travel $\left(\dfrac{x}{2} - 5\right) + \left(\dfrac{x}{2} + 4\frac{3}{4}\right)$ in the same time that the train travels $(2x - 1) + (3x - \frac{1}{4})$. These two periods of time reduce to $(x - \frac{1}{4})$ and $5(x - \frac{1}{4})$, so we see that the train is five times faster than the cow. With this information we write the equation:

$$2x - 1 = 5\left(\dfrac{x}{2} - 5\right).$$

This gives x, the length of the bridge, a value of 48 feet. The actual speed of the train plays no part whatever in this calculation, but we need to know it in order to learn the speed of the cow. Since we are told that the train traveled at 90 miles per hour, we know the cow's gait to be 18 miles per hour.

SELECTED REFERENCES

Chess Strategy: a Treatise upon the Art of Problem Composi-tion, by Sam Loyd, 1878. Privately published: Elizabeth, N. J. A collection of about 500 of Loyd's chess problems.

Sam Loyd and His Chess Problems, by Alain C. White, 1913. Whitehead and Miller: Leeds, England. A major source of biographical information on Loyd.

Sam Loyd's Puzzles: a Book for Children, edited by Sam Loyd II, 1912. David McKay: Philadelphia.

Sam Loyd's Cyclopedia of 5000 Puzzles, Tricks, and Conun-drums, edited by Sam Loyd II, 1914. The Lamb Publishing Company: New York.

Sam Loyd's Picture Puzzles, edited by Sam Loyd II, 1924. Privately printed: New York.

Sam Loyd and His Puzzles, edited by Sam Loyd II, 1928, Barse and Company: New York.

"The Prince of Puzzle Makers," by George C. Bain. *The Strand Magazine*, December, 1907.

"My Fifty Years in Puzzleland," by Walted P. Eaton. *Delinea-tor*, April, 1911.

"Geometrical Vanishes," Chapters 7 and 8, *Mathematics, Magic, and Mystery*, by Martin Gardner, 1956. Dover Pub-lications: New York. A detailed discussion of Loyd's "Get off the Earth" puzzle and related paradoxes.

"Sam Loyd: America's Greatest Puzzlist," Chapter 9, *The Scientific American Book of Mathematical Puzzles and Diversions*, 1959. Simon and Schuster: New York. Includes reproductions of Loyd's original "Trick Donkeys" and "Teddy and the Lions" puzzles.

Catalog
of
DOVER BOOKS

BOOKS EXPLAINING SCIENCE

(Note: The books listed under this category are general introductions, surveys, reviews, and non-technical expositions of science for the interested layman or scientist who wishes to brush up. Dover also publishes the largest list of inexpensive reprints of books on intermediate and higher mathematics, mathematical physics, engineering, chemistry, astronomy, etc., for the professional mathematician or scientist. For our complete Science Catalog, write Dept. catrr., Dover Publications, Inc., 180 Varick Street, New York 14, N. Y.)

CONCERNING THE NATURE OF THINGS, Sir William· Bragg. Royal Institute Christmas Lectures by Nobel Laureate. Excellent plain-language introduction to gases, molecules, crystal structure, etc. explains "building blocks" of universe, basic properties of matter, with simplest, clearest examples, demonstrations. 32pp. of photos; 57 figures. 244pp. 5⅜ x 8.
T31 Paperbound **$1.35**

MATTER AND LIGHT, THE NEW PHYSICS, Louis de Broglie. Non-technical explanations by a Nobel Laureate of electro-magnetic theory, relativity, wave mechanics, quantum physics, philosophies of science, etc. Simple, yet accurate introduction to work of Planck, Bohr, Einstein, other modern physicists. Only 2 of 12 chapters require mathematics. 300pp. 5⅜ x 8.
T35 Paperbound **$1.60**

THE COMMON ·SENSE OF THE EXACT SCIENCES, W. K. Clifford. For 70 years, Clifford's work has been acclaimed as one of the clearest, yet most precise introductions to mathematical symbolism, measurement, surface boundaries, position, space, motion, mass and force, etc. Prefaces by Bertrand Russell and Karl Pearson. Introduction by James Newman. 130 figures. 249pp. 5⅜ x 8.
T61 Paperbound **$1.60**

THE NATURE OF LIGHT AND COLOUR IN THE OPEN AIR, M. Minnaert. What causes mirages? haloes? "multiple" suns and moons? Professor Minnaert explains these and hundreds of other fascinating natural optical phenomena in simple terms, tells how to observe them, suggests hundreds of experiments. 200 illus; 42 photos. xvi + 362pp.
T196 Paperbound **$1⸱95**

SPINNING TOPS AND GYROSCOPIC MOTION, John Perry. Classic elementary text on dynamics of rotation treats gyroscopes, tops, how quasi-rigidity is induced in paper disks, smoke rings, chains, etc, by rapid motion, precession, earth's motion, etc. Contains many easy-to-perform experiments. Appendix on practical uses of gyroscopes. 62 figures. 128pp.
T416 Paperbound **$1.00**

A CONCISE HISTORY OF MATHEMATICS, D. Struik. This lucid, easily followed history of mathematics from the Ancient Near East to modern times requires no mathematical background itself, yet introduces both mathematicians and laymen to basic concepts and discoveries and the men who made them. Contains a collection of 31 portraits of eminent mathematicians. Bibliography. xix + 299pp. 5⅜ x 8. T255 Paperbound **$1.75**

THE RESTLESS UNIVERSE, Max Born. A remarkably clear, thorough exposition of gases, electrons, ions, waves and particles, electronic structure of the atom, nuclear physics, written for the layman by a Nobel Laureate. "Much ·more thorough and deep than most attempts . . . easy and delightful," CHEMICAL AND ENGINEERING NEWS. Includes 7 animated sequences showing motion of molecules, alpha particles, etc. 11 full-page plates of photographs. Total of nearly 600 illus. 315pp. 6⅛ x 9¼. T412 Paperbound **$2.00**

WHAT IS SCIENCE?, N. Campbell. The role of experiment, the function of mathematics, the nature of scientific laws, the limitations of science, and many other provocative topics are explored without technicalities by an eminent scientist. "Still an excellent introduction to scientific philosophy," H. Margenau in PHYSICS TODAY. 192pp. 5⅜ x 8.
S43 Paperbound **$1.25**

FADS AND FALLACIES IN THE NAME OF SCIENCE, Martin Gardner. The standard account of the various cults, quack systems and delusions which have recently masqueraded as science: hollow earth theory, Atlantis, dianetics, Reich's orgone theory, flying saucers, Bridey Murphy, psionics, irridiagnosis, many other fascinating fallacies that deluded tens of thousands. "Should be read by everyone, scientist and non-scientist alike," R. T. Birge, Prof. Emeritus, Univ. of California; Former President, American Physical Society. Formerly titled, "In the Name of Science." Revised and enlarged edition. x + 365pp. 5⅜ x 8.
T394 Paperbound **$1.50**

THE STUDY OF THE HISTORY OF MATHEMATICS, THE STUDY OF THE HISTORY OF SCIENCE, G. Sarton. Two books bound as one. Both volumes are standard introductions to their fields by an eminent science historian. They discuss problems of historical research, teaching, pitfalls, other matters of interest to the historically oriented writer, teacher, or student. Both have extensive bibliographies. 10 illustrations. 188pp. 5⅜ x 8.
T240 Paperbound **$1.25**

THE PRINCIPLES OF SCIENCE, W. S. Jevons. Unabridged reprinting of a milestone in the development of symbolic logic and other subjects concerning scientific methodology, probability, inferential validity, etc. Also describes Jevons' "logic machine," an early precursor of modern electronic calculators. Preface by E. Nagel. 839pp. 5⅜ x 8. S446 Paperbound **$2.98**

SCIENCE THEORY AND MAN, Erwin Schroedinger. Complete, unabridged reprinting of "Science and the Human Temperament" plus an additional essay "What is an Elementary Particle?" Nobel Laureate Schroedinger discusses many aspects of modern physics from novel points of view which provide unusual insights for both laymen and physicists. 192 pp. 5⅜ x 8.
T428 Paperbound **$1.35**

BRIDGES AND THEIR BUILDERS, D. B. Steinman & S. R. Watson. Information about ancient, medieval, modern bridges; how they were built; who built them; the structural principles employed; the materials they are built of; etc. Written by one of the world's leading authorities on bridge design and construction. New, revised, expanded edition. 23 photos; 26 line drawings, xvii + 401pp. 5⅜ x 8.
T431 Paperbound **$1.95**

HISTORY OF MATHEMATICS, D. E. Smith. Most comprehensive non-technical history of math in English. In two volumes. Vol. I: A chronological examination of the growth of mathematics from primitive concepts up to 1900. Vol. II: The development of ideas in specific fields and areas, up through elementary calculus. The lives and works of over a thousand mathematicians are covered; thousands of specific historical problems and their solutions are clearly explained. Total of 510 illustrations, 1355pp. 5⅜ x 8. Set boxed in attractive container.
T429, T430 Paperbound, the set **$5.00**

PHILOSOPHY AND THE PHYSICISTS, L. S. Stebbing. A philosopher examines the philosophical implications of modern science by posing a lively critical attack on the popular science expositions of Sir James Jeans and Arthur Eddington. xvi + 295pp. 5⅜ x 8.
T480 Paperbound **$1.65**

ON MATHEMATICS AND MATHEMATICIANS, R. E. Moritz. The first collection of quotations by and about mathematicians in English. 1140 anecdotes, aphorisms, definitions, speculations, etc. give both mathematicians and layman stimulating new insights into what mathematics is, and into the personalities of the great mathematicians from Archimedes to Euler, Gauss, Klein, Weierstrass. Invaluable to teachers, writers. Extensive cross index. 410pp. 5⅜ x 8.
T489 Paperbound **$1.95**

NATURAL SCIENCE, BIOLOGY, GEOLOGY, TRAVEL

A SHORT HISTORY OF ANATOMY AND PHYSIOLOGY FROM THE GREEKS TO HARVEY, C. Singer. A great medical historian's fascinating intermediate account of the slow advance of anatomical and physiological knowledge from pre-scientific times to Vesalius, Harvey. 139 unusually interesting illustrations. 221pp. 5⅜ x 8.
T389 Paperbound **$1.75**

THE BEHAVIOUR AND SOCIAL LIFE OF HONEYBEES, Ronald Ribbands. The most comprehensive, lucid and authoritative book on bee habits, communication, duties, cell life, motivations, etc. "A MUST for every scientist, experimenter, and educator, and a happy and valuable selection for all interested in the honeybee," AMERICAN BEE JOURNAL. 690-item bibliography. 127 illus.; 11 photographic plates. 352pp. 5⅜ x 8⅜. S410 Clothbound **$4.50**

TRAVELS OF WILLIAM BARTRAM, edited by Mark Van Doren. One of the 18th century's most delightful books, and one of the few first-hand sources of information about American geography, natural history, and anthropology of American Indian tribes of the time. "The mind of a scientist with the soul of a poet," John Livingston Lowes. 13 original illustrations, maps. Introduction by Mark Van Doren. 448pp. 5⅜ x 8. T326 Paperbound **$2.00**

STUDIES ON THE STRUCTURE AND DEVELOPMENT OF VERTEBRATES, Edwin Goodrich. The definitive study of the skeleton, fins and limbs, head region, divisions of the body cavity, vascular, respiratory, excretory systems, etc., of vertebrates from fish to higher mammals, by the greatest comparative anatomist of recent times. "The standard textbook," JOURNAL OF ANATOMY. 754 illus. 69-page biographical study. 1186-item bibliography. 2 vols. Total of 906pp. 5⅜ x 8.
Vol. I: S449 Paperbound **$2.50**
Vol. II: S450 Paperbound **$2.50**

DOVER BOOKS

THE BIRTH AND DEVELOPMENT OF THE GEOLOGICAL SCIENCES, F. D. Adams. The most complete and thorough history of the earth sciences in print. Covers over 300 geological thinkers and systems; treats fossils, theories of stone growth, paleontology, earthquakes, vulcanists vs. neptunists, odd theories, etc. 91 illustrations, including medieval, Renaissance wood cuts, etc. 632 footnotes and bibliographic notes. 511pp. 308pp. 5⅜ x 8.   T5 Paperbound **$2.00**

FROM MAGIC TO SCIENCE, Charles Singer. A close study of aspects of medical science from the Roman Empire through the Renaissance. The sections on early herbals, and "The Visions of Hildegarde of Bingen," are probably the best studies of these subjects available. 158 unusual classic and medieval illustrations. xxvii + 365pp. 5⅜ x 8.   T390 Paperbound **$2.00**

SAILING ALONE AROUND THE WORLD, Captain Joshua Slocum. Captain Slocum's personal account of his single-handed voyage around the world in a 34-foot boat he rebuilt himself. A classic of both seamanship and descriptive writing. "A nautical equivalent of Thoreau's account," Van Wyck Brooks. 67 illus. 308pp. 5⅜ x 8.   T326 Paperbound **$1.00**

TREES OF THE EASTERN AND CENTRAL UNITED STATES AND CANADA, W. M. Harlow. Standard middle-level guide designed to help you know the characteristics of Eastern trees and identify them at sight by means of an 8-page synoptic key. More than 600 drawings and photographs of twigs, leaves, fruit, other features. xiii + 288pp. 4⅝ x 6½.
T395 Paperbound **$1.35**

FRUIT KEY AND TWIG KEY ("Fruit Key to Northeastern Trees," "Twig Key to Deciduous Woody Plants of Eastern North America"), **W. M. Harlow.** Identify trees in fall, winter, spring. Easy-to-use, synoptic keys, with photographs of every twig and fruit identified. Covers 120 different fruits, 160 different twigs. Over 350 photos. Bibliographies. Glossaries. Total of 143pp. 5⅝ x 8⅜.   T511 Paperbound **$1.25**

INTRODUCTION TO THE STUDY OF EXPERIMENTAL MEDICINE, Claude Bernard. This classic records Bernard's far-reaching efforts to transform physiology into an exact science. It covers problems of vivisection, the limits of physiological experiment, hypotheses in medical experimentation, hundreds of others. Many of his own famous experiments on the liver, the pancreas, etc., are used as examples. Foreword by I. B. Cohen. xxv + 266pp. 5⅜ x 8.
T400 Paperbound **$1.50**

THE ORIGIN OF LIFE, A. I. Oparin. The first modern statement that life evolved from complex nitro-carbon compounds, carefully presented according to modern biochemical knowledge of primary colloids, organic molecules, etc. Begins with historical introduction to the problem of the origin of life. Bibliography. xxv + 270pp. 5⅜ x 8.   S213 Paperbound **$1.75**

A HISTORY OF ASTRONOMY FROM THALES TO KEPLER, J. L. E. Dreyer. The only work in English which provides a detailed picture of man's cosmological views from Egypt, Babylonia, Greece, and Alexandria to Copernicus, Tycho Brahe and Kepler. "Standard reference on Greek astronomy and the Copernican revolution," SKY AND TELESCOPE. Formerly called "A History of Planetary Systems From Thales to Kepler." Bibliography. 21 diagrams. xvii + 430pp. 5⅜ x 8.
S79 Paperbound **$1.98**

URANIUM PROSPECTING, H. L. Barnes. A professional geologist tells you what you need to know. Hundreds of facts about minerals, tests, detectors, sampling, assays, claiming, developing, government regulations, etc. Glossary of technical terms. Annotated bibliography. x + 117pp. 5⅜ x 8.   T309 Paperbound **$1.00**

DE RE METALLICA, Georgius Agricola. All 12 books of this 400 year old classic on metals and metal production, fully annotated, and containing all 289 of the 16th century woodcuts which made the original an artistic masterpiece. A superb gift for geologists, engineers, libraries, artists, historians. Translated by Herbert Hoover & L. H. Hoover. Bibliography, survey of ancient authors. 289 illustrations of the excavating, assaying, smelting, refining, and countless other metal production operations described in the text. 672pp. 6¾ x 10¾. Deluxe library edition.   S6 Clothbound **$10.00**

DE MAGNETE, William Gilbert. A landmark of science by the man who first used the word "electricity," distinguished between static electricity and magnetism, and founded a new science. P. F. Mottelay translation. 90 figures. lix + 368pp. 5⅜ x 8.   S470 Paperbound **$2.00**

THE AUTOBIOGRAPHY OF CHARLES DARWIN AND SELECTED LETTERS, Francis Darwin, ed. Fascinating documents on Darwin's early life, the voyage of the "Beagle," the discovery of evolution, Darwin's thought on mimicry, plant development, vivisection, evolution, many other subjects Letters to Henslow, Lyell, Hooker, Wallace, Kingsley, etc. Appendix. 365pp. 5⅜ x 8.   T479 Paperbound **$1.65**

A WAY OF LIFE AND OTHER SELECTED WRITINGS OF SIR WILLIAM OSLER. 16 of the great physician, teacher and humanist's most inspiring writings on a practical philosophy of life, science and the humanities, and the history of medicine. 5 photographs. Introduction by G. L. Keynes, M.D., F.R.C.S. xx + 278pp. 5⅜ x 8.   T488 Paperbound **$1.50**

LITERATURE

WORLD DRAMA, B. H. Clark. 46 plays from Ancient Greece, Rome, to India, China, Japan. Plays by Aeschylus, Sophocles, Euripides, Aristophanes, Plautus, Marlowe, Jonson, Farquhar, Goldsmith, Cervantes, Molière, Dumas, Goethe, Schiller, Ibsen, many others. One of the most comprehensive collections of important plays from all literature available in English. Over ⅓ of this material is unavailable in any other current edition. Reading lists. 2 volumes. Total of 1364pp. 5⅜ x 8.　　　　　　　　　　　　　　Vol. I, T57 Paperbound **$2.00**
　　　　　　　　　　　　　　　　　　　　　　　　　　　Vol. II, T59 Paperbound **$2.00**

MASTERS OF THE DRAMA, John Gassner. The most comprehensive history of the drama in print. Covers more than 800 dramatists and over 2000 plays from the Greeks to modern Western, Near Eastern, Oriental drama. Plot summaries, theatre history, etc. "Best of its kind in English," NEW REPUBLIC. 35 pages of bibliography. 77 photos and drawings. Deluxe edition. xxii + 890pp. 5⅜ x 8.　　　　　　　　　　　　　T100 Clothbound **$5.95**

THE DRAMA OF LUIGI PIRANDELLO, D. Vittorini. All 38 of Pirandello's plays (to 1935) summarized and analyzed in terms of symbolic techniques, plot structure, etc. The only authorized work. Foreword by Pirandello. Biography. Bibliography. xiii + 350pp. 5⅜ x 8.
　　　　　　　　　　　　　　　　　　　　　　　　　T435 Paperbound **$1.98**

ARISTOTLE'S THEORY OF POETRY AND THE FINE ARTS, S. H. Butcher, ed. The celebrated "Butcher translation" faced page by page with the Greek text; Butcher's 300-page introduction to Greek poetic, dramatic thought. Modern Aristotelian criticism discussed by John Gassner. lxxvi + 421pp. 5⅜ x 8.

　　　　　　　　　　　　　　　　　　　　　　　　　　T42 Paperbound **$2.00**

EUGENE O'NEILL: THE MAN AND HIS PLAYS, B. H. Clark. The first published source-book on O'Neill's life and work. Analyzes each play from the early THE WEB up to THE ICEMAN COMETH. Supplies much information about environmental and dramatic influences. ix + 182pp. 5⅜ x 8.　　　　　　　　　　　　　　　　　　　　T379 Paperbound **$1.25**

INTRODUCTION TO ENGLISH LITERATURE, B. Dobrée, ed. Most compendious literary aid in its price range. Extensive, categorized bibliography (with entries up to 1949) of more than 5,000 poets, dramatists, novelists, as well as historians, philosophers, economists, religious writers, travellers, and scientists of literary stature. Information about manuscripts, important biographical data. Critical, historical, background works not simply listed, but evaluated. Each volume also contains a long introduction to the period it covers.

Vol. I: **THE BEGINNINGS OF ENGLISH LITERATURE TO SKELTON, 1509, W. L. Renwick. H. Orton.** 450pp. 5⅛ x 7⅛.　　　　　　　　　　　　　　　　　T75 Clothbound **$3.50**

Vol. II: **THE ENGLISH RENAISSANCE, 1510-1688, V. de Sola Pinto.** 381pp. 5⅛ x 7⅛.
　　　　　　　　　　　　　　　　　　　　　　　　　　T76 Clothbound **$3.50**

Vol. III: **THE AUGUSTANS AND ROMANTICS, 1689-1830, H. Dyson, J. Butt.** 320pp. 5⅛ x 7⅛.
　　　　　　　　　　　　　　　　　　　　　　　　　　T77 Clothbound **$3.50**

Vol. IV: **THE VICTORIANS AND AFTER, 1830-1914, E. Batho, B. Dobrée.** 360pp. 5⅛ x 7⅛.
　　　　　　　　　　　　　　　　　　　　　　　　　　T78 Clothbound **$3.50**

EPIC AND ROMANCE, W. P. Ker. The standard survey of Medieval epic and romance by a foremost authority on Medieval literature. Covers historical background, plot, literary analysis, significance of Teutonic epics, Icelandic sagas, Beowulf, French chansons de geste, the Niebelungenlied, Arthurian romances, much more. 422pp. 5⅜ x 8.　　T355 Paperbound **$1.95**

THE HEART OF EMERSON'S JOURNALS, Bliss Perry, ed. Emerson's most intimate thoughts, impressions, records of conversations with Channing, Hawthorne, Thoreau, etc., carefully chosen from the 10 volumes of The Journals. "The essays do not reveal the power of Emerson's mind . . .as do these hasty and informal writings," N. Y. TIMES. Preface by B. Perry. 370pp. 5⅜ x 8.　　　　　　　　　　　　　　　　T447 Paperbound **$1.85**

A SOURCE BOOK IN THEATRICAL HISTORY, A. M. Nagler. (Formerly, "Sources of Theatrical History.") Over 300 selected passages by contemporary observers tell about styles of acting, direction, make-up, scene designing, etc., in the theatre's great periods from ancient Greece to the Théâtre Libre. "Indispensable complement to the study of drama," EDUCATIONAL THEATRE JOURNAL. Prof. Nagler, Yale Univ. School of Drama, also supplies notes, references. 85 illustrations. 611pp. 5⅜ x 8.　　　　　　　　　　　　　T515 Paperbound **$2.75**

THE ART OF THE STORY-TELLER, M. L. Shedlock. Regarded as the finest, most helpful book on telling stories to children, by a great story-teller. How to catch, hold, recapture attention; how to choose material; many other aspects. Also includes: a 99-page selection of Miss Shedlock's most successful stories; extensive bibliography of other stories. xxi + 320pp. 5⅜ x 8.　　　　　　　　　　　　　　　　　　　　　T245 Clothbound **$3.50**

THE DEVIL'S DICTIONARY, Ambrose Bierce. Over 1000 short, ironic definitions in alphabetical order, by America's greatest satirist in the classical tradition. "Some of the most gorgeous witticisms in the English language," H. L. Mencken. 144pp. 5⅜ x 8.　　T487 Paperbound **$1.00**

MUSIC

A DICTIONARY OF HYMNOLOGY, John Julian. More than 30,000 entries on individual hymns, their authorship, textual variations, location of texts, dates and circumstances of composition, denominational and ritual usages, the biographies of more than 9,000 hymn writers, essays on important topics such as children's hymns and Christmas carols, and hundreds of thousands of other important facts about hymns which are virtually impossible to find anywhere else. Convenient alphabetical listing, and a 200-page double-columned index of first lines enable you to track down virtually any hymn ever written. Total of 1786pp. 6¼ x 9¼. 2 volumes.   T133. The Set, Clothbound **$15.00**

STRUCTURAL HEARING, TONAL COHERENCE IN MUSIC, Felix Salzer. Extends the well-known Schenker approach to include modern music, music of the middle ages, and Renaissance music. Explores the phenomenon of tonal organization by discussing more than 500 compositions, and offers unusual new insights into the theory of composition and musical relationships. "The foundation on which all teaching in music theory has been based at this college," Leopold Mannes, President, The Mannes College of Music. Total of 658pp. 6½ x 9¼. 2 volumes.   S418 The set, Clothbound **$8.00**

A GENERAL HISTORY OF MUSIC, Charles Burney. The complete history of music from the Greeks up to 1789 by the 18th century musical historian who personally knew the great Baroque composers. Covers sacred and secular, vocal and instrumental, operatic and symphonic music; treats theory, notation, forms, instruments; discusses composers, performers, important works. Invaluable as a source of information on the period for students, historians, musicians. "Surprisingly few of Burney's statements have been invalidated by modern research . . . still of great value," NEW YORK TIMES. Edited and corrected by Frank Mercer. 35 figures. 1915pp. 5½ x 8½. 2 volumes.   T36 The set, Clothbound **$12.50**

JOHANN SEBASTIAN BACH, Phillip Spitta. Recognized as one of the greatest accomplishments of musical scholarship and far and away the definitive coverage of Bach's works. Hundreds of individual pieces are analyzed. Major works, such as the B Minor Mass and the St. Matthew Passion are examined in minute detail. Spitta also deals with the works of Buxtehude, Pachelbel, and others of the period. Can be read with profit even by those without a knowledge of the technicalities of musical composition. "Unchallenged as the last word on one of the supreme geniuses of music," John Barkham, SATURDAY REVIEW SYNDICATE. Total of 1819pp. 5⅜ x 8. 2 volumes.   T252 The set, Clothbound **$10.00**

HISTORY

THE IDEA OF PROGRESS, J. B. Bury. Prof. Bury traces the evolution of a central concept of Western civilization in Greek, Roman, Medieval, and Renaissance thought to its flowering in the 17th and 18th centuries. Introduction by Charles Beard. xl + 357pp. 5⅜ x 8.
T39 Clothbound **$3.95**
T40 Paperbound **$1.95**

THE ANCIENT GREEK HISTORIANS, J. B. Bury. Greek historians such as Herodotus, Thucydides, Xenophon; Roman historians such as Tacitus, Caesar, Livy; scores of others fully analyzed in terms of sources, concepts, influences, etc., by a great scholar and historian. 291pp. 5⅜ x 8.   T397 Paperbound **$1.50**

HISTORY OF THE LATER ROMAN EMPIRE, J. B. Bury. The standard work on the Byzantine Empire from 395 A.D. to the death of Justinian in 565 A.D., by the leading Byzantine scholar of our time. Covers political, social, cultural, theological, military history. Quotes contemporary documents extensively. "Most unlikely that it will ever be superseded," Glanville Downey, Dumbarton Oaks Research Library. Genealogical tables. 5 maps. Bibliography. 2 vols. Total of 965pp. 5⅜ x 8.   T398, T399 Paperbound, the set **$4.00**

GARDNER'S PHOTOGRAPHIC SKETCH BOOK OF THE CIVIL WAR, Alexander Gardner. One of the rarest and most valuable Civil War photographic collections exactly reproduced for the first time since 1866. Scenes of Manassas, Bull Run, Harper's Ferry, Appomattox, Mechanicsville, Fredericksburg, Gettysburg, etc.; battle ruins, prisons, arsenals, a slave pen, fortifications; Lincoln on the field, officers, men, corpses. By one of the most famous pioneers in documentary photography. Original copies of the "Sketch Book" sold for $425 in 1952. Introduction by E. Bleiler. 100 full-page 7 x 10 photographs (original size). 244pp. 10¾ x 8½.
T476 Clothbound **$6.00**

THE WORLD'S GREAT SPEECHES, L. Copeland and L. Lamm, eds. 255 speeches from Pericles to Churchill, Dylan Thomas. Invaluable as a guide to speakers; fascinating as history past and present; a source of much difficult-to-find material. Includes an extensive section of informal and humorous speeches. 3 indices: Topic, Author, Nation. xx + 745pp. 5⅜ x 8.
T468 Paperbound **$2.49**

FOUNDERS OF THE MIDDLE AGES, E. K. Rand. The best non-technical discussion of the transformation of Latin paganism into medieval civilization. Tertullian, Gregory, Jerome, Boethius, Augustine, the Neoplatonists, other crucial figures, philosophies examined. Excellent for the intelligent non-specialist. "Extraordinarily accurate," Richard McKeon, THE NATION. ix + 365pp. 5⅜ x 8.   T369 Paperbound **$1.85**

THE POLITICAL THOUGHT OF PLATO AND ARISTOTLE, Ernest Barker. The standard, comprehensive exposition of Greek political thought. Covers every aspect of the "Republic" and the "Politics" as well as minor writings, other philosophers, theorists of the period, and the later history of Greek political thought. Unabridged edition. 584pp. 5⅜ x 8.
T521 Paperbound **$1.85**

PHILOSOPHY

THE GIFT OF LANGUAGE, M. Schlauch. (Formerly, "The Gift of Tongues.") A sound, middle-level treatment of linguistic families, word histories, grammatical processes, semantics, language taboos, word-coining of Joyce, Cummings, Stein, etc. 232 bibliographical notes. 350pp. 5⅜ x 8.
T243 Paperbound **$1.85**

THE PHILOSOPHY OF HEGEL, W. T. Stace. The first work in English to give a complete and connected view of Hegel's entire system. Especially valuable to those who do not have time to study the highly complicated original texts, yet want an accurate presentation by a most reputable scholar of one of the most influential 19th century thinkers. Includes a 14 x 20 fold-out chart of Hegelian system. 536pp. 5⅜ x 8.
T254 Paperbound **$2.00**

ARISTOTLE, A. E. Taylor. A lucid, non-technical account of Aristotle written by a foremost Platonist. Covers life and works; thought on matter, form, causes, logic, God, physics, metaphysics, etc. Bibliography. New index compiled for this edition. 128pp. 5⅜ x 8.
T280 Paperbound **$1.00**

GUIDE TO PHILOSOPHY, C. E. M. Joad. This basic work describes the major philosophic problems and evaluates the answers propounded by great philosophers from the Greeks to Whitehead, Russell. "The finest introduction," BOSTON TRANSCRIPT. Bibliography, 592pp. 5⅜ x 8.
T297 Paperbound **$2.00**

LANGUAGE AND MYTH, E. Cassirer. Cassirer's brilliant demonstration that beneath both language and myth lies an unconscious "grammar" of experience whose categories and canons are not those of logical thought. Introduction and translation by Susanne Langer. Index. x + 103pp. 5⅜ x 8.
T51 Paperbound **$1.25**

SUBSTANCE AND FUNCTION, EINSTEIN'S THEORY OF RELATIVITY, E. Cassirer. This double volume contains the German philosopher's profound philosophical formulation of the differences between traditional logic and the new logic of science. Number, space, energy, relativity, many other topics are treated in detail. Authorized translation by W. C. and M. C. Swabey. xii + 465pp. 5⅜ x 8.
T50 Paperbound **$2.00**

THE PHILOSOPHICAL WORKS OF DESCARTES. The definitive English edition, in two volumes, of all major philosophical works and letters of René Descartes, father of modern philosophy of knowledge and science. Translated by E. S. Haldane and G. Ross. Introductory notes. Total of 842pp. 5⅜ x 8.
T71 Vol. 1, Paperbound **$2.00**
T72 Vol. 2, Paperbound **$2.00**

ESSAYS IN EXPERIMENTAL LOGIC, J. Dewey. Based upon Dewey's theory that knowledge implies a judgment which in turn implies an inquiry, these papers consider such topics as the thought of Bertrand Russell, pragmatism, the logic of values, antecedents of thought, data and meanings. 452pp. 5⅜ x 8.
T73 Paperbound **$1.95**

THE PHILOSOPHY OF HISTORY, G. W. F. Hegel. This classic of Western thought is Hegel's detailed formulation of the thesis that history is not chance but a rational process, the realization of the Spirit of Freedom. Translated and introduced by J. Sibree. Introduction by C. Hegel. Special introduction for this edition by Prof. Carl Friedrich, Harvard University. xxxix + 447pp. 5⅜ x 8.
T112 Paperbound **$1.85**

THE WILL TO BELIEVE and HUMAN IMMORTALITY, W. James. Two of James's most profound investigations of human belief in God and immortality, bound as one volume. Both are powerful expressions of James's views on chance vs. determinism, pluralism vs. monism, will and intellect, arguments for survival after death, etc. Two prefaces. 429pp. 5⅜ x 8.
T294 Clothbound **$3.75**
T291 Paperbound **$1.65**

INTRODUCTION TO SYMBOLIC LOGIC, S. Langer. A lucid, general introduction to modern logic, covering forms, classes, the use of symbols, the calculus of propositions, the Boole-Schroeder and the Russell-Whitehead systems, etc. "One of the clearest and simplest introductions," MATHEMATICS GAZETTE. Second, enlarged, revised edition. 368pp. 5⅜ x 8.
S164 Paperbound **$1.75**

MIND AND THE WORLD-ORDER, C. I. Lewis. Building upon the work of Peirce, James, and Dewey, Professor Lewis outlines a theory of knowledge in terms of "conceptual pragmatism," and demonstrates why the traditional understanding of the a priori must be abandoned. Appendices. xiv + 446pp. 5⅜ x 8.
T359 Paperbound **$1.95**

THE GUIDE FOR THE PERPLEXED, M. Maimonides One of the great philosophical works of all time, Maimonides' formulation of the meeting-ground between Old Testament and Aristotelian thought is essential to anyone interested in Jewish, Christian, and Moslem thought in the Middle Ages. 2nd revised edition of the Friedländer translation. Extensive introduction. lix + 414pp. 5⅜ x 8.
T351 Paperbound **$1.85**

DOVER BOOKS

THE PHILOSOPHICAL WRITINGS OF PEIRCE, J. Buchler, ed. (Formerly, "The Philosophy of Peirce.") This carefully integrated selection of Peirce's papers is considered the best coverage of the complete thought of one of the greatest philosophers of modern times. Covers Peirce's work on the theory of signs, pragmatism, epistemology, symbolic logic, the scientific method, chance, etc. xvi + 386pp. 5 ⅜ x 8.   T216 Clothbound **$5.00**
                                                                                                        T217 Paperbound **$1.95**

HISTORY OF ANCIENT PHILOSOPHY, W. Windelband. Considered the clearest survey of Greek and Roman philosophy. Examines Thales, Anaximander, Anaximenes, Heraclitus, the Eleatics, Empedocles, the Pythagoreans, the Sophists, Socrates, Democritus, Stoics, Epicureans, Sceptics, Neo-platonists, etc. 50 pages on Plato; 70 on Aristotle. 2nd German edition tr. by H. E. Cushman. xv + 393pp. 5⅜ x 8.   T357 Paperbound **$1.75**

INTRODUCTION TO SYMBOLIC LOGIC AND ITS APPLICATIONS, R. Carnap. A comprehensive, rigorous introduction to modern logic by perhaps its greatest living master. Includes demonstrations of applications in mathematics, physics, biology. "Of the rank of a masterpiece," Z. für Mathematik und ihre Grenzgebiete. Over 300 exercises. xvi + 241pp. 5⅜ x 8.   Clothbound **$4.00**
                                                                                                        S453 Paperbound **$1.85**

SCEPTICISM AND ANIMAL FAITH, G. Santayana. Santayana's unusually lucid exposition of the difference between the independent existence of objects and the essence our mind attributes to them, and of the necessity of scepticism as a form of belief and animal faith as a necessary condition of knowledge. Discusses belief, memory, intuition, symbols, etc. xii + 314pp. 5⅜ x 8.   T235 Clothbound **$3.50**
                                                                                                        T236 Paperbound **$1.50**

THE ANALYSIS OF MATTER, B. Russell. With his usual brilliance, Russell analyzes physics, causality, scientific inference, Weyl's theory, tensors, invariants, periodicity, etc. in order to discover the basic concepts of scientific thought about matter. "Most thorough treatment of the subject," THE NATION. Introduction. 8 figures. viii + 408pp. 5⅜ x 8.
                                                                                                        T231 Paperbound **$1.95**

THE SENSE OF BEAUTY, G. Santayana. This important philosophical study of why, when, and how beauty appears, and what conditions must be fulfilled, is in itself a revelation of the beauty of language. "It is doubtful if a better treatment of the subject has since appeared," PEABODY JOURNAL. ix + 275pp. 5⅜ x 8.   T238 Paperbound **$1.00**

THE CHIEF WORKS OF SPINOZA. In two volumes. Vol. I: The Theologico-Political Treatise and the Political Treatise. Vol. II: On the Improvement of Understanding, The Ethics, and Selected Letters. The permanent and enduring ideas in these works on God, the universe, religion, society, etc., have had tremendous impact on later philosophical works. Introduction. Total of 862pp. 5⅜ x 8.   T249 Vol. I, Paperbound **$1.50**
                                                                                                        T250 Vol. II, Paperbound **$1.50**

TRAGIC SENSE OF LIFE, M. de Unamuno. The acknowledged masterpiece of one of Spain's most influential thinkers. Between the despair at the inevitable death of man and all his works, and the desire for immortality, Unamuno finds a "saving incertitude." Called "a masterpiece," by the ENCYCLOPAEDIA BRITANNICA. xxx + 332pp. 5⅜ x 8.
                                                                                                        T257 Paperbound **$1.95**

EXPERIENCE AND NATURE, John Dewey. The enlarged, revised edition of the Paul Carus lectures (1925). One of Dewey's clearest presentations of the philosophy of empirical naturalism which reestablishes the continuity between "inner" experience and "outer" nature. These lectures are among the most significant ever delivered by an American philosopher. 457pp. 5⅜ x 8.   T471 Paperbound **$1.85**

PHILOSOPHY AND CIVILIZATION IN THE MIDDLE AGES, M. de Wulf. A semi-popular survey of medieval intellectual life, religion, philosophy, science, the arts, etc. that covers feudalism vs. Catholicism, rise of the universities, mendicant orders, and similar topics. Bibliography. viii + 320pp. 5⅜ x 8.   T284 Paperbound **$1.75**

AN INTRODUCTION TO SCHOLASTIC PHILOSOPHY, M. de Wulf. (Formerly, "Scholasticism Old and New.") Prof. de Wulf covers the central scholastic tradition from St. Anselm, Albertus Magnus, Thomas Aquinas, up to Suarez in the 17th century; and then treats the modern revival of scholasticism, the Louvain position, relations with Kantianism and positivism, etc. xvi + 271pp. 5⅜ x 8.   T296 Clothbound **$3.50**
                                                                                                        T283 Paperbound **$1.75**

A HISTORY OF MODERN PHILOSOPHY, H. Höffding. An exceptionally clear and detailed coverage of Western philosophy from the Renaissance to the end of the 19th century. Both major and minor figures are examined in terms of theory of knowledge, logic, cosmology, psychology. Covers Pomponazzi, Bodin, Boehme, Telesius, Bruno, Copernicus, Descartes, Spinoza, Hobbes, Locke, Hume, Kant, Fichte, Schopenhauer, Mill, Spencer, Langer, scores of others. A standard reference work. 2 volumes. Total of 1159pp. 5⅜ x 8.   T117 Vol. 1, Paperbound **$2.00**
                                                                                                        T118 Vol. 2, Paperbound **$2.00**

LANGUAGE, TRUTH AND LOGIC, A. J. Ayer. The first full-length development of Logical Positivism in English. Building on the work of Schlick, Russell, Carnap, and the Vienna school, Ayer presents the tenets of one of the most important systems of modern philosophical thought. 160pp. 5⅜ x 8.   T10 Paperbound **$1.25**

ORIENTALIA AND RELIGION

THE MYSTERIES OF MITHRA, F. Cumont. The great Belgian scholar's definitive study of the Persian mystery religion that almost vanquished Christianity in the ideological struggle for the Roman Empire. A masterpiece of scholarly detection that reconstructs secret doctrines, organization, rites. Mithraic art is discussed and analyzed. 70 illus. 239pp. 5⅜ x 8.
T323 Paperbound **$1.85**

CHRISTIAN AND ORIENTAL PHILOSOPHY OF ART. A. K. Coomaraswamy. The late art historian and orientalist discusses artistic symbolism, the role of traditional culture in enriching art, medieval art, folklore, philosophy of art, other similar topics. Bibliography. 148pp. 5⅜ x 8.
T378 Paperbound **$1.25**

TRANSFORMATION OF NATURE IN ART, A. K. Coomaraswamy. A basic work on Asiatic religious art. Includes discussions of religious art in Asia and Medieval Europe (exemplified by Meister Eckhart), the origin and use of images in Indian art, Indian Medieval aesthetic manuals, and other fascinating, little known topics. Glossaries of Sanskrit and Chinese terms. Bibliography. 41pp. of notes. 245pp. 5⅜ x 8.
T368 Paperbound **$1.75**

ORIENTAL RELIGIONS IN ROMAN PAGANISM, F. Cumont. This well-known study treats the ecstatic cults of Syria and Phrygia (Cybele, Attis, Adonis, their orgies and mutilatory rites); the mysteries of Egypt (Serapis, Isis, Osiris); Persian dualism; Mithraic cults; Hermes Trismegistus, Ishtar, Astarte, etc. and their influence on the religious thought of the Roman Empire. Introduction. 55pp. of notes; extensive bibliography. xxiv + 298pp. 5⅜ x 8.
T321 Paperbound **$1.75**

ANTHROPOLOGY, SOCIOLOGY, AND PSYCHOLOGY

PRIMITIVE MAN AS PHILOSOPHER, P. Radin. A standard anthropological work based on Radin's investigations of the Winnebago, Maori, Batak, Zuni, other primitive tribes. Describes primitive thought on the purpose of life, marital relations, death, personality, gods, etc. Extensive selections of original primitive documents. Bibliography. xviii + 420pp. 5⅜ x 8.
T392 Paperbound **$2.00**

PRIMITIVE RELIGION, P. Radin. Radin's thoroughgoing treatment of supernatural beliefs, shamanism, initiations, religious expression, etc. in primitive societies. Arunta, Ashanti, Aztec, Bushman, Crow, Fijian, many other tribes examined. "Excellent," NATURE. New preface by the author. Bibliographic notes. x + 322pp. 5⅜ x 8.   T393 Paperbound **$1.85**

SEX IN PSYCHO-ANALYSIS, S. Ferenczi. (Formerly, "Contributions to Psycho-analysis.") 14 selected papers on impotence, transference, analysis and children, dreams, obscene words, homosexuality, paranoia, etc. by an associate of Freud. Also included: THE DEVELOPMENT OF PSYCHO-ANALYSIS, by Ferenczi and Otto Rank. Two books bound as one. Total of 406pp. 5⅜ x 8.   T324 Paperbound **$1.85**

THE PRINCIPLES OF PSYCHOLOGY, William James. The complete text of the famous "long course," one of the great books of Western thought. An almost incredible amount of information about psychological processes, the stream of consciousness, habit, time perception, memory, emotions, reason, consciousness of self, abnormal phenomena, and similar topics. Based on James's own discoveries integrated with the work of Descartes, Locke, Hume, Royce, Wundt, Berkeley, Lotse, Herbart, scores of others. "A classic of interpretation," PSYCHIATRIC QUARTERLY. 94 illus. 1408pp. 2 volumes. 5⅜ x 8.
T381 Vol. 1, Paperbound **$2.50**
T382 Vol. 2, Paperbound **$2.50**

THE POLISH PEASANT IN EUROPE AND AMERICA, W. I. Thomas, F. Znaniecki. Monumental sociological study of peasant primary groups (family and community) and the disruptions produced by a new industrial system and emigration to America, by two of the foremost sociologists of recent times. One of the most important works in sociological thought. Includes hundreds of pages of primary documentation; point by point analysis of causes of social decay, breakdown of morality, crime, drunkenness, prostitution, etc. 2nd revised edition. 2 volumes. Total of 2250pp. 6 x 9.   T478 2 volume set, Clothbound **$12.50**

FOLKWAYS, W. G. Sumner. The great Yale sociologist's detailed exposition of thousands of social, sexual, and religious customs in hundreds of cultures from ancient Greece to Modern Western societies. Preface by A. G. Keller. Introduction by William Lyon Phelps. 705pp. 5⅜ x 8.   S508 Paperbound **$2.49**

BEYOND PSYCHOLOGY, Otto Rank. The author, an early associate of Freud, uses psychoanalytic techniques of myth-analysis to explore ultimates of human existence. Treats love, immortality, the soul, sexual identity, kingship, sources of state power, many other topics which illuminate the irrational basis of human existence. 291pp. 5⅜ x 8.   T485 Paperbound **$1.75**

ILLUSIONS AND DELUSIONS OF THE SUPERNATURAL AND THE OCCULT, D. H. Rawcliffe. A rational, scientific examination of crystal gazing, automatic writing, table turning, stigmata, the Indian rope trick, dowsing, telepathy, clairvoyance, ghosts, ESP, PK, thousands of other supposedly occult phenomena. Originally titled "The Psychology of the Occult." 14 illustrations. 551pp. 5⅜ x 8.   T503 Paperbound **$2.00**

DOVER BOOKS

YOGA: A SCIENTIFIC EVALUATION, Kovoor T. Behanan. A scientific study of the physiological and psychological effects of Yoga discipline, written under the auspices of the Yale University Institute of Human Relations. Foreword by W. A. Miles, Yale Univ. 17 photographs. 290pp. 5⅜ x 8.   T505 Paperbound **$1.65**

HOAXES, C. D. MacDougall. Delightful, entertaining, yet scholarly exposition of how hoaxes start, why they succeed, documented with stories of hundreds of the most famous hoaxes. "A stupendous collection . . . and shrewd analysis, "NEW YORKER. New, revised edition. 54 photographs. 320pp. 5⅜ x 8.   T465 Paperbound **$1.75**

CREATIVE POWER: THE EDUCATION OF YOUTH IN THE CREATIVE ARTS, Hughes Mearns. Named by the National Education Association as one of the 20 foremost books on education in recent times. Tells how to help children express themselves in drama, poetry, music, art, develop latent creative power. Should be read by every parent, teacher. New, enlarged, revised edition. Introduction. 272pp. 5⅜ x 8.   T490 Paperbound **$1.50**

LANGUAGES

NEW RUSSIAN-ENGLISH, ENGLISH-RUSSIAN DICTIONARY, M. A. O'Brien. Over 70,000 entries in new orthography! Idiomatic usages, colloquialisms. One of the few dictionaries that indicate accent changes in conjugation and declension. "One of the best," Prof. E. J. Simmons, Cornell. First names, geographical terms, bibliography, many other features. 738pp. 4½ x 6¼.   T208 Paperbound **$2.00**

MONEY CONVERTER AND TIPPING GUIDE FOR EUROPEAN TRAVEL, C. Vomacka. Invaluable, handy source of currency regulations, conversion tables, tipping rules, postal rates, much other travel information for every European country plus Israel, Egypt and Turkey. 128pp. 3½ x 5¼.   T260 Paperbound **60¢**

MONEY CONVERTER AND TIPPING GUIDE FOR TRAVEL IN THE AMERICAS (including the United States and Canada), **C. Vomacka.** The information you need for informed and confident travel in the Americas: money conversion tables, tipping guide, postal, telephone rates, etc. 128pp. 3½ x 5¼.   T261 Paperbound **65¢**

DUTCH-ENGLISH, ENGLISH-DUTCH DICTIONARY, F. G. Renier. The most convenient, practical Dutch-English dictionary on the market. New orthography. More than 60,000 entries: idioms, compounds, technical terms, etc. Gender of nouns indicated. xviii + 571pp. 5½ x 6¼.   T224 Clothbound **$2.50**

LEARN DUTCH!, F. G. Renier. The most satisfactory and easily-used grammar of modern Dutch. Used and recommended by the Fulbright Committee in the Netherlands. Over 1200 simple exercises lead to mastery of spoken and written Dutch. Dutch-English, English-Dutch vocabularies. 181pp. 4¼ x 7¼.   T441 Clothbound **$1.75**

PHRASE AND SENTENCE DICTIONARY OF SPOKEN RUSSIAN, English-Russian, Russian-English. Based on phrases and complete sentences, rather than isolated words; recognized as one of the best methods of learning the idiomatic speech of a country. Over 11,500 entries, indexed by single words, with more than 32,000 English and Russian sentences and phrases, in immediately usable form. Probably the largest list ever published. Shows accent changes in conjugation and declension; irregular forms listed in both alphabetical place and under main form of word. 15,000 word introduction covering Russian sounds, writing, grammar, syntax. 15-page appendix of geographical names, money, important signs, given names, foods, special Soviet terms, etc. Travellers, businessmen, students, government employees have found this their best source for Russian expressions. Originally published as U.S. Government Technical Manual TM 30-944. iv + 573pp. 5⅝ x 8⅜.   T496 Paperbound **$2.75**

PHRASE AND SENTENCE DICTIONARY OF SPOKEN SPANISH, Spanish-English, English-Spanish. Compiled from spoken Spanish, emphasizing idiom and colloquial usage in both Castilian and Latin-American. More than 16,000 entries containing over 25,000 idioms—the largest list of idiomatic constructions ever published. Complete sentences given, indexed under single words —language in immediately usable form, for travellers, businessmen, students, etc. 25-page introduction provides rapid survey of sounds, grammar, syntax, with full consideration of irregular verbs. Especially apt in modern treatment of phrases and structure. 17-page glossary gives translations of geographical names, money values, numbers, national holidays, important street signs, useful expressions of high frequency, plus unique 7-page glossary of Spanish and Spanish-American foods and dishes. Originally published as U.S. Government Technical Manual TM 30-900. iv + 513pp. 5⅝ x 8⅜.   T495 Paperbound **$1.75**

SAY IT language phrase books

"SAY IT" in the foreign language of your choice! We have sold over ½ million copies of these popular, useful language books. They will not make you an expert linguist overnight, but they do cover most practical matters of everyday life abroad.

Over 1000 useful phrases, expressions, with additional variants, substitutions.

Modern! Useful! Hundreds of phrases not available in other texts: "Nylon," "air-conditioned," etc.

The ONLY inexpensive phrase book **completely indexed.** Everything is available at a flip of your finger, ready for use.

Prepared by native linguists, travel experts.

Based on years of travel experience abroad.

This handy phrase book may be used by itself, or it may supplement any other text or course; it provides a living element. Used by many colleges and institutions: Hunter College; Barnard College; Army Ordnance School, Aberdeen; and many others.

Available, 1 book per language:

Danish (T818) 75¢
Dutch T(817) 75¢
English (for German-speaking people) (T801) 60¢
English (for Italian-speaking people) (T816) 60¢
English (for Spanish-speaking people) (T802) 60¢
Esperanto (T820) 75¢
French (T803) 60¢
German (T804) 60¢
Modern Greek (T813) 75¢
Hebrew (T805) 60¢

Italian (T806) 60¢
Japanese (T807) 60¢
Norwegian (T814) 75¢
Russian (T810) 75¢
Spanish (T811) 60¢
Turkish (T821) 75¢
Yiddish (T815) 75¢
Swedish (T812) 75¢
Polish (T808) 75¢
Portuguese (T809) 75¢

LISTEN & LEARN language record sets

LISTEN & LEARN is the only language record course designed especially to meet your travel needs, or help you learn essential foreign language quickly by yourself, or in conjunction with any school course, by means of the automatic association method. Each set contains three 33⅓ rpm long-playing records — 1½ hours of recorded speech by eminent native speakers who are professors at Columbia, N.Y.U., Queens College and other leading universities. The sets are priced far below other sets of similar quality, yet they contain many special features not found in other record sets:

* Over 800 selected phrases and sentences, a basic vocabulary of over 3200 words.
* Both English and foreign language recorded; with a pause for your repetition.
* Designed for persons with limited time; no time wasted on material you cannot use immediately.
* Living, modern expressions that answer modern needs: drugstore items, "air-conditioned," etc.
* 128-196 page manuals contain everything on the records, plus simple pronunciation guides.
* Manual is fully indexed; find the phrase you want instantly.
* High fidelity recording—equal to any records costing up to $6 each.

The phrases on these records cover 41 different categories useful to the traveller or student interested in learning the living, spoken language: greetings, introductions, making yourself understood, passing customs, planes, trains, boats, buses, taxis, nightclubs, restaurants, menu items, sports, concerts, cameras, automobile travel, repairs, drugstores, doctors, dentists, medicines, barber shops, beauty parlors, laundries, many, many more.

"Excellent . . . among the very best on the market," Prof. Mario Pei, Dept. of Romance Languages, Columbia University. "Inexpensive and well-done . . . an ideal present," CHICAGO SUNDAY TRIBUNE. "More genuinely helpful than anything of its kind which I have previously encountered," Sidney Clark, well-known author of "ALL THE BEST" travel books. Each set contains 3 33⅓ rpm pure vinyl records, 128-196 page with full record text, and album. One language per set. LISTEN & LEARN record sets are now available in—

FRENCH	the set $4.95		**GERMAN**	the set $4.95
ITALIAN	the set $4.95		**SPANISH**	the set $4.95
RUSSIAN	the set $5.95		**JAPANESE** *	the set $5.95

* Available Sept. 1, 1959

UNCONDITIONAL GUARANTEE: Dover Publications stands behind every Listen and Learn record set. If you are dissatisfied with these sets for any reason whatever, return them within 10 days and your money will be refunded in full.

DOVER BOOKS

ART HISTORY

STICKS AND STONES, Lewis Mumford. An examination of forces influencing American architecture: the medieval tradition in early New England, the classical influence in Jefferson's time, the Brown Decades, the imperial facade, the machine age, etc. "A truly remarkable book," SAT. REV. OF LITERATURE. 2nd revised edition. 21 illus. xvii + 228pp. 5⅜ x 8.
T202 Paperbound **$1.60**

THE AUTOBIOGRAPHY OF AN IDEA, Louis Sullivan. The architect whom Frank Lloyd Wright called "the master," records the development of the theories that revolutionized America's skyline. 34 full-page plates of Sullivan's finest work. New introduction by R. M. Line. xiv + 335pp. 5⅜ x 8.
T281 Paperbound **$1.85**

THE MATERIALS AND TECHNIQUES OF MEDIEVAL PAINTING, D. V. Thompson. An invaluable study of carriers and grounds, binding media, pigments, metals used in painting, al fresco and al secco techniques, burnishing, etc. used by the medieval masters. Preface by Bernard Berenson. 239pp. 5⅜ x 8.
T327 Paperbound **$1.85**

PRINCIPLES OF ART HISTORY, H. Wölfflin. This remarkably instructive work demonstrates the tremendous change in artistic conception from the 14th to the 18th centuries, by analyzing 164 works by Botticelli, Dürer, Hobbema, Holbein, Hals, Titian, Rembrandt, Vermeer, etc., and pointing out exactly what is meant by "baroque," "classic," "primitive," "picturesque," and other basic terms of art history and criticism. "A remarkable lesson in the art of seeing," SAT. REV. OF LITERATURE. Translated from the 7th German edition. 150 illus. 254pp. 6⅛ x 9¼.
T276 Paperbound **$2.00**

FOUNDATIONS OF MODERN ART, A. Ozenfant. Stimulating discussion of human creativity from paleolithic cave painting to modern painting, architecture, decorative arts. Fully illustrated with works of Gris, Lipchitz, Leger, Picasso, primitive, modern artifacts, architecture, industrial art, much more. 226 illustrations. 368pp. 6⅛ x 9¼.
T215 Paperbound **$1.95**

HANDICRAFTS, APPLIED ART, ART SOURCES, ETC.

WILD FOWL DECOYS, J. Barber. The standard work on this fascinating branch of folk art, ranging from Indian mud and grass devices to realistic wooden decoys. Discusses styles, types, periods; gives full information on how to make decoys. 140 illustrations (including 14 new plates) show decoys and provide full sets of plans for handicrafters, artists, hunters, and students of folk art. 281pp. 7⅞ x 10¾. Deluxe edition.
T11 Clothbound **$8.50**

METALWORK AND ENAMELLING, H. Maryon. Probably the best book ever written on the subject. Tells everything necessary for the home manufacture of jewelry, rings, ear pendants, bowls, etc. Covers materials, tools, soldering, filigree, setting stones, raising patterns, repoussé work, damascening, niello, cloisonné, polishing, assaying, casting, and dozens of other techniques. The best substitute for apprenticeship to a master metalworker. 363 photos and figures. 374pp. 5½ x 8½.
T183 Clothbound **$7.50**

SHAKER FURNITURE, E. D. and F. Andrews. The most illuminating study of Shaker furniture ever written. Covers chronology, craftsmanship, houses, shops, etc. Includes over 200 photographs of chairs, tables, clocks, beds, benches, etc. "Mr. & Mrs. Andrews know all there is to know about Shaker furniture," Mark Van Doren, NATION. 48 full-page plates. 192pp. Deluxe cloth binding. 7⅞ x 10¾.
T7 Clothbound **$6.00**

PRIMITIVE ART, Franz Boas. A great American anthropologist covers theory, technical virtuosity, styles, symbolism, patterns, etc. of primitive art. The more than 900 illustrations will interest artists, designers, craftworkers. Over 900 illustrations. 376pp. 5⅜ x 8.
T25 Paperbound **$1.95**

ON THE LAWS OF JAPANESE PAINTING, H. Bowie. The best possible substitute for lessons from an oriental master. Treats both spirit and technique; exercises for control of the brush; inks, brushes, colors; use of dots, lines to express whole moods, etc. 220 illus. 132pp. 6⅛ x 9¼.
T30 Paperbound **$1.95**

HANDBOOK OF ORNAMENT, F. S. Meyer. One of the largest collections of copyright-free traditional art: over 3300 line cuts of Greek, Roman, Medieval, Renaissance, Baroque, 18th and 19th century art motifs (tracery, geometric elements, flower and animal motifs, etc.) and decorated objects (chairs, thrones, weapons, vases, jewelry, armor, etc.). Full text. 3300 illustrations. 562pp. 5⅜ x 8.
T302 Paperbound **$2.00**

THREE CLASSICS OF ITALIAN CALLIGRAPHY. Oscar Ogg, ed. Exact reproductions of three famous Renaissance calligraphic works: Arrighi's OPERINA and IL MODO, Tagliente's LO PRESENTE LIBRO, and Palatino's LIBRO NUOVO. More than 200 complete alphabets, thousands of lettered specimens, in Papal Chancery and other beautiful, ornate handwriting. Introduction. 245 plates. 282pp. 6⅛ x 9¼.
T212 Paperbound **$1.95**

THE HISTORY AND TECHNIQUES OF LETTERING, A. Nesbitt. A thorough history of lettering from the ancient Egyptians to the present, and a 65-page course in lettering for artists. Every major development in lettering history is illustrated by a complete alphabet. Fully analyzes such masters as Caslon, Koch, Garamont, Jenson, and many more. 89 alphabets, 165 other specimens. 317pp. 5⅜ x 8.
T427 Paperbound **$2.00**

LETTERING AND ALPHABETS, J. A. Cavanagh. An unabridged reissue of "Lettering," containing the full discussion, analysis, illustration of 89 basic hand lettering tyles based on Caslon, Bodoni, Gothic, many other types. Hundreds of technical hints on construction, strokes, pens, brushes, etc. 89 alphabets, 72 lettered specimens, which may be reproduced permission-free. 121pp. 9¾ x 8. T53 Paperbound **$1.25**

THE HUMAN FIGURE IN MOTION, Eadweard Muybridge. The largest collection in print of Muybridge's famous high-speed action photos. 4789 photographs in more than 500 action-strip-sequences (at shutter speeds up to 1/6000th of a second) illustrate men, women, children—mostly undraped—performing such actions as walking, running, getting up, lying down, carrying objects, throwing, etc. "An unparalleled dictionary of action for all artists," AMERICAN ARTIST. 390 full-page plates, with 4789 photographs. Heavy glossy stock, reinforced binding with headbands. 7⅞ x 10¾. T204 Clothbound **$10.00**

ANIMALS IN MOTION, Eadweard Muybridge. The largest collection of animal action photos in print. 34 different animals (horses, mules, oxen, goats, camels, pigs, cats, lions, gnus, deer, monkeys, eagles—and 22 others) in 132 characteristic actions. All 3919 photographs are taken in series at speeds up to 1/1600th of a second, offering artists, biologists, cartoonists a remarkable opportunity to see exactly how an ostrich's head bobs when running, how a lion puts his foot down, how an elephant's knee bends, how a bird flaps his wings, thousands of other hard-to-catch details. "A really marvelous series of plates," NATURE. 380 full-pages of plates. Heavy glossy stock, reinforced binding with headbands. 7⅞ x10¾. T203 Clothbound **$10.00**

THE BOOK OF SIGNS, R. Koch. 493 symbols—crosses, monograms, astrological, biological symbols, runes, etc.—from ancient manuscripts, cathedrals, coins, catacombs, pottery. May be reproduced permission-free. 493 illustrations by Fritz Kredel. 104pp. 6⅛ x 9¼. T162 Paperbound **$1.00**

A HANDBOOK OF EARLY ADVERTISING ART, C. P. Hornung. The largest collection of copyright-free early advertising art ever compiled. Vol. I: 2,000 illustrations of animals, old automobiles, buildings, allegorical figures, fire engines, Indians, ships, trains, more than 33 other categories! Vol II: Over 4,000 typographical specimens; 600 Roman, Gothic, Barnum, Old English faces; 630 ornamental type faces; hundreds of scrolls, initials, flourishes, etc. "A remarkable collection," PRINTERS' INK.

Vol. I: Pictorial Volume. Over 2000 illustrations. 256pp. 9 x 12. T122 Clothbound **$10.00**
Vol. II: Typographical Volume. Over 4000 specimens. 319pp. 9 x 12. T123 Clothbound **$10.00**
Two volume set, Clothbound, only **$18.50**

DESIGN FOR ARTISTS AND CRAFTSMEN, L. Wolchonok. The most thorough course on the creation of art motifs and designs. Shows you step-by-step, with hundreds of examples and 113 detailed exercises, how to create original designs from geometric patterns, plants, birds, animals, humans, and man-made objects. "A great contribution to the field of design and crafts," N. Y. SOCIETY OF CRAFTSMEN. More than 1300 entirely new illustrations. xv + 207pp. 7⅞ x 10¾. T274 Clothbound **$4.95**

HANDBOOK OF DESIGNS AND DEVICES, C. P. Hornung. A remarkable working collection of 1836 basic designs and variations, all copyright-free. Variations of circle, line, cross, diamond, swastika, star, scroll, shield, many more. Notes on symbolism. "A necessity to every designer who would be original without having to labor heavily," ARTIST and ADVERTISER. 204 plates. 240pp. 5⅜ x 8. T125 Paperbound **$1.90**

THE UNIVERSAL PENMAN, George Bickham. Exact reproduction of beautiful 18th century book of handwriting. 22 complete alphabets in finest English roundhand, other scripts, over 2000 elaborate flourishes, 122 calligraphic illustrations, etc. Material is copyright-free. "An essential part of any art library, and a book of permanent value," AMERICAN ARTIST. 212 plates. 224pp. 9 x 13¾. T20 Clothbound **$10.00**

AN ATLAS OF ANATOMY FOR ARTISTS, F. Schider. This standard work contains 189 full-page plates, more than 647 illustrations of all aspects of the human skeleton, musculature, cutaway portions of the body, each part of the anatomy, hand forms, eyelids, breasts, location of muscles under the flesh, etc. 59 plates illustrate how Michelangelo, da Vinci, Goya, 15 others, drew human anatomy. New 3rd edition enlarged by 52 new illustrations by Cloquet, Barcsay. "The standard reference tool," AMERICAN LIBRARY ASSOCIATION. "Excellent," AMERICAN ARTIST. 189 plates, 647 illustrations. xxvi + 192pp. 7⅞ x 10⅝. T241 Clothbound **$6.00**

AN ATLAS OF ANIMAL ANATOMY FOR ARTISTS, W. Ellenberger, H. Baum, H. Dittrich. The largest, richest animal anatomy for artists in English. Form, musculature, tendons, bone structure, expression, detailed cross sections of head, other features, of the horse, lion, dog, cat, deer, seal, kangaroo, cow, bull, goat, monkey, hare, many other animals. "Highly recommended," DESIGN. Second, revised, enlarged edition with new plates from Cuvier, Stubbs, etc. 288 illustrations. 153pp. 11⅜ x 9. T82 Clothbound **$6.00**

ANIMAL DRAWING: ANATOMY AND ACTION FOR ARTISTS, C. R. Knight. 158 studies, with full accompanying text, of such animals as the gorilla, bear, bison, dromedary, camel, vulture, pelican, iguana, shark, etc., by one of the greatest modern masters of animal drawing. Innumerable tips on how to get life expression into your work. "An excellent reference work,' SAN FRANCISCO CHRONICLE. 158 illustrations. 156pp. 10½ x 8½. T426 Paperbound **$2.00**

THE CRAFTSMAN'S HANDBOOK, Cennino Cennini. The finest English translation of IL LIBRO DELL' ARTE, the 15th century introduction to art technique that is both a mirror of Quatrocento life and a source of many useful but ·nearly forgotten facets of the painter's art. 4 illustrations. xxvii + 142pp. D. V. Thompson, translator. 6⅛ x 9¼.　　T54 Paperbound **$1.50**

THE BROWN DECADES, Lewis Mumford. A picture of the "buried renaissance" of the post-Civil War period, and the founding of modern architecture (Sullivan, Richardson, Root, Roebling), landscape development (Marsh, Olmstead, Eliot), and the graphic arts (Homer, Eakins, Ryder). 2nd revised, enlarged edition. Bibliography. 12 illustrations. xiv + 266 pp. 5⅜ x 8.　　T200 Paperbound **$1.65**

STIEGEL GLASS, F. W. Hunter. The story of the most highly esteemed early American glassware, fully illustrated. How a German adventurer, "Baron" Stiegel, founded a glass empire; detailed accounts of individual glasswork. "This pioneer work is reprinted in an edition even more beautiful than the original," ANTIQUES DEALER. New introduction by Helen McKearin. 171 illustrations, 12 in full color. xxii + 338pp. 7⅞ x 10¾.
　　T128 Clothbound **$10.00**

THE HUMAN FIGURE, J. H. Vanderpoel. Not just a picture book, but a complete course by a famous figure artist. Extensive text, illustrated by 430 pencil and charcoal drawings of both male and female anatomy. 2nd enlarged edition. Foreword. 430 illus. 143pp. 6⅛ x 9¼.
　　T432 Paperbound **$1.45**

PINE FURNITURE OF EARLY NEW ENGLAND, R. H. Kettell. Over 400 illustrations, over 50 working drawings of early New England chairs, benches, beds cupboards, mirrors, shelves, tables, other furniture esteemed for simple beauty and character. "Rich store of illustrations . . . emphasizes the individuality and varied design," ANTIQUES. 413 illustrations, 55 working drawings. 475pp. 8 x 10¾.　　T145 Clothbound **$10.00**

BASIC BOOKBINDING, A. W. Lewis. Enables both beginners and experts to rebind old books or bind paperbacks in hard covers. Treats materials, tools; gives step-by-step instruction in how to collate a book, sew it, back it, make boards, etc. 261 illus. Appendices. 155pp. 5⅜ x 8.　　T169 Paperbound **$1.35**

DESIGN MOTIFS OF ANCIENT MEXICO, J. Enciso. Nearly 90% of these 766 superb designs from Aztec, Olmec, Totonac, Maya, and Toltec origins are unobtainable elsewhere! Contains plumed serpents, wind gods, animals, demons, dancers, monsters, etc. Excellent applied design source. Originally $17.50. 766 illustrations, thousands of motifs. 192pp. 6⅛ x 9¼.
　　T84 Paperbound **$1.85**

AFRICAN SCULPTURE, Ladislas Segy. 163 full-page plates illustrating masks, fertility figures, ceremonial objects, etc., of 50 West and Central African tribes—95% never before illustrated. 34-page introduction to African sculpture. "Mr. Segy is one of its top authorities," NEW YORKER. 164 full-page photographic plates. Introduction. Bibliography. 244pp. 6⅛ x 9¼.
　　T396 Paperbound **$2.00**

THE PROCESSES OF GRAPHIC REPRODUCTION IN PRINTING, H. Curwen. A thorough and practical survey of wood, linoleum, and rubber engraving; copper engraving; drypoint, mezzotint, etching, aquatint, steel engraving, die sinking, stencilling, lithography (extensively); photographic reproduction utilizing line, continuous tone, photoengravure, collotype; every other process in general use. Note on color reproduction. Section on bookbinding. Over 200 illustrations, 25 in color. 143pp. 5½ x 8½.　　T512 Clothbound **$4.00**

CALLIGRAPHY, J. G. Schwandner. First reprinting in 200 years of this legendary book of beautiful handwriting. Over 300 ornamental initials, 12 complete calligraphic alphabets, over 150 ornate frames and panels, 75 calligraphic pictures of cherubs, stags, lions, etc., thousands of flourishes, scrolls, etc., by the greatest 18th century masters. All material can be copied or adapted without permission. Historical introduction. 158 full-page plates. 368pp. 9 x 13.　　T475 Clothbound **$10.00**

* * *

A DIDEROT PICTORIAL ENCYCLOPEDIA OF TRADES AND INDUSTRY, Manufacturing and the Technical Arts in Plates Selected from "L'Encyclopédie ou Dictionnaire Raisonné des Sciences, des Arts, et des Métiers," of Denis Diderot, edited with text by C. Gillispie. Over 2000 illustrations on 485 full-page plates. Magnificent 18th century engravings of men, women, and children working at such trades as milling flour, cheesemaking, charcoal burning, mining, silverplating, shoeing horses, making fine glass, printing, hundreds more, showing details of machinery, different steps in sequence, etc. A remarkable art work, but also the largest collection of working figures in print, copyright-free, for art directors, designers, etc. Two vols. 920pp. 9 x 12. Heavy library cloth.　　T421 Two volume set **$18.50**

* * *

SILK SCREEN TECHNIQUES, J. Biegeleisen, M. Cohn. A practical step-by-step home course in one of the most versatile, least expensive graphic arts processes. How to build an inexpensive silk screen, prepare stencils, print, achieve special textures, use color, etc. Every step explained, diagrammed. 149 illustrations, 8 in color. 201pp. 6⅛ x 9¼.
　　T433 Paperbound **$1.45**

PUZZLES, GAMES, AND ENTERTAINMENTS

MATHEMATICS, MAGIC AND MYSTERY, Martin Gardner. Astonishing feats of mind reading, mystifying "magic" tricks, are often based on mathematical principles anyone can learn. This book shows you how to perform scores of tricks with cards, dice, coins, knots, numbers, etc., by using simple principles from set theory, theory of numbers, topology, other areas of mathematics, fascinating in themselves. No special knowledge required. 135 illus. 186pp. 5⅜ x 8.   T335 Paperbound **$1.00**

MATHEMATICAL PUZZLES FOR BEGINNERS AND ENTHUSIASTS, G. Mott-Smoth. Test your problem-solving techniques and powers of inference on 188 challenging, amusing puzzles based on algebra, dissection of plane figures, permutations, probabilities, etc. Appendix of primes, square roots, etc. 135 illus. 2nd revised edition. 248pp. 5⅜ x 8.
T198 Paperbound **$1.00**

LEARN CHESS FROM THE MASTERS, F. Reinfeld. Play 10 games against Marshall, Bronstein, Najdorf, other masters, and grade yourself on each move. Detailed annotations reveal principles of play, strategy, etc. as you proceed. An excellent way to get a real insight into the game. Formerly titled, "Chess by Yourself." 91 diagrams. vii + 144pp. 5⅜ x 8.
T362 Paperbound **$1.00**

REINFELD ON THE END GAME IN CHESS, F. Reinfeld. 62 end games of Alekhine, Tarrasch, Morphy, other masters, are carefully analyzed with emphasis on transition from middle game to end play. Tempo moves, queen endings, weak squares, other basic principles clearly illustrated. Excellent for understanding why some moves are weak or incorrect, how to avoid errors. Formerly titled, "Practical End-game Play." 62 diagrams. vi + 177pp. 5⅜ x 8.
T417 Paperbound **$1.25**

101 PUZZLES IN THOUGHT AND LOGIC, C. R. Wylie, Jr. Brand new puzzles you need no special knowledge to solve! Each one is a gem of ingenuity that will really challenge your problem-solving technique. Introduction with simplified explanation of scientic puzzle solving. 128pp. 5⅜ x 8.   T167 Paperbound **$1.00**

THE COMPLETE NONSENSE OF EDWARD LEAR. The only complete edition of this master of gentle madness at a popular price. The Dong with the Luminous Nose, The Jumblies, The Owl and the Pussycat, hundreds of other bits of wonderful nonsense. 214 limericks, 3 sets of Nonsense Botany, 5 Nonsense Alphabets, 546 fantastic drawings, much more. 320pp. 5⅜ x 8.   T167 Paperbound **$1.00**

28 SCIENCE FICTION STORIES OF H. G. WELLS. Two complete novels, "Men Like Gods" and "Star Begotten," plus 26 short stories by the master science-fiction writer of all time. Stories of space, time, future adventure that are among the all-time classics of science fiction. 928pp. 5⅜ x 8.   T265 Clothbound **$3.95**

SEVEN SCIENCE FICTION NOVELS, H. G. Wells. Unabridged texts of "The Time Machine," "The Island of Dr. Moreau," "First Men in the Moon," "The Invisible Man," "The War of the Worlds," "The Food of the Gods," "In the Days of the Comet." "One will have to go far to match this for entertainment, excitement, and sheer pleasure," N. Y. TIMES. 1015pp. 5⅜ x 8.   T264 Clothbound **$3.95**

MATHEMAGIC, MAGIC PUZZLES, AND GAMES WITH NUMBERS, R. V. Heath. More than 60 new puzzles and stunts based on number properties: multiplying large numbers mentally, finding the date of any day in the year, etc. Edited by J. S. Meyer. 76 illus. 129pp. 5⅜ x 8.
T110 Paperbound **$1.00**

FIVE ADVENTURE NOVELS OF H. RIDER HAGGARD. The master story-teller's five best tales of mystery and adventure set against authentic African backgrounds: "She," "King Solomon's Mines," "Allan Quatermain," "Allan's Wife," "Maiwa's Revenge." 821pp. 5⅜ x 8.
T108 Clothbound **$3.95**

WIN AT CHECKERS, M. Hopper. (Formerly "Checkers.") The former World's Unrestricted Checker Champion gives you valuable lessons in openings, traps, end games, ways to draw when you are behind, etc. More than 100 questions and answers anticipate your problems. Appendix. 75 problems diagrammed, solved. 79 figures. xi + 107pp. 5⅜ x 8.
T363 Paperbound **$1.00**

CRYPTOGRAPHY, L. D. Smith. Excellent introductory work on ciphers and their solution, history of secret writing, techniques, etc. Appendices on Japanese methods, the Baconian cipher, frequency tables. Bibliography. Over 150 problems, solutions. 160pp. 5⅜ x 8.
T247 Paperbound **$1.00**

CRYPTANALYSIS, H. F. Gaines. (Formerly, "Elementary Cryptanalysis.") The best book available on cryptograms and how to solve them. Contains all major techniques: substitution, transposition, mixed alphabets, multafid, Kasiski and Vignere methods, etc. Word frequency appendix. 167 problems, solutions. 173 figures. 236pp. 5⅜ x 8.   T97 Paperbound **$1.95**

FLATLAND, E. A. Abbot. The science-fiction classic of life in a 2-dimensional world that is considered a first-rate introduction to relativity and hyperspace, as well as a scathing satire on society, politics and religion. 7th edition. 16 illus. 128pp. 5⅜ x 8.
T1 Paperbound **$1.00**

DOVER BOOKS

HOW TO FORCE CHECKMATE, F. Reinfeld. (Formerly "Challenge to Chessplayers.") No board needed to sharpen your checkmate skill on 300 checkmate situations. Learn to plan up to 3 moves ahead and play a superior end game. 300 situations diagrammed; notes and full solutions. 111pp. 5⅜ x 8.   T439 Paperbound **$1.25**

MORPHY'S GAMES OF CHESS, P. W. Sergeant, ed. Play forcefully by following the techniques used by one of the greatest chess champions. 300 of Morphy's games carefully annotated to reveal principles. Bibliography. New introduction by F. Reinfeld. 235 diagrams. x + 352pp. 5⅜ x 8.   T386 Paperbound **$1.75**

MATHEMATICAL RECREATIONS, M. Kraitchik. Hundreds of unusual mathematical puzzlers and odd bypaths of math, elementary and advanced. Greek, Medieval, Arabic, Hindu problems; figurate numbers, Fermat numbers, primes; magic, Euler, Latin squares; fairy chess, latruncles, reversi, jinx, ruma, tetrachrome other positional and permutational games. Rigorous solutions. Revised second edition. 181 illus. 330pp. 5⅜ x 8.   T163 Paperbound **$1.75**

MATHEMATICAL EXCURSIONS, H. A. Merrill. Revealing stimulating insights into elementary math, not usually taught in school. 90 problems demonstrate Russian peasant multiplication, memory systems for pi, magic squares, dyadic systems, division by inspection, many more. Solutions to difficult problems. 50 illus. 5⅜ x 8.   T350 Paperbound **$1.00**

MAGIC TRICKS & CARD TRICKS, W. Jonson. Best introduction to tricks with coins, bills, eggs, ribbons, slates, cards, easily performed without elaborate equipment. Professional routines, tips on presentation, misdirection, etc. Two books bound as one: 52 tricks with cards, 37 tricks with common objects. 106 figures. 224pp. 5⅜ x 8.   T909 Paperbound **$1.00**

MATHEMATICAL PUZZLES OF SAM LOYD, selected and edited by **M. Gardner.** 177 most ingenious mathematical puzzles of America's greatest puzzle originator, based on arithmetic, algebra, game theory, dissection, route tracing, operations research, probability, etc. 120 drawings, diagrams. Solutions. 187pp. 5⅜ x 8.   T498 Paperbound **$1.00**

THE ART OF CHESS, J. Mason. The most famous general study of chess ever written. More than 90 openings, middle game, end game, how to attack, sacrifice, defend, exchange, form general strategy. Supplement on "How Do You Play Chess?" by F. Reinfeld. 448 diagrams. 356pp. 5⅜ x 8.   T463 Paperbound **$1.85**

HYPERMODERN CHESS as Developed in the Games of its Greatest Exponent, ARON NIMZOVICH, F. Reinfeld, ed. Learn how the game's greatest innovator defeated Alekhine, Lasker, and many others; and use these methods in your own game. 180 diagrams. 228pp. 5⅜ x 8.
                                                             T448 Paperbound **$1.35**

A TREASURY OF CHESS LORE, F. Reinfeld, ed. Hundreds of fascinating stories by and about the masters, accounts of tournaments and famous games, aphorisms, word portraits, little known incidents, photographs, etc., that will delight the chess enthusiast, captivate the beginner. 49 photographs (14 full-page plates), 12 diagrams. 315pp. 5⅜ x 8.
                                                             T458 Paperbound **$1.75**

A NONSENSE ANTHOLOGY, collected by **Carolyn Wells.** 245 of the best nonsense verses ever written: nonsense puns, absurd arguments, mock epics, nonsense ballads, "sick" verses, dog-Latin verses, French nonsense verses, limericks. Lear, Carroll, Belloc, Burgess, nearly 100 other writers. Introduction by Carolyn Wells. 3 indices: Title, Author, First Lines. xxxiii + 279pp. 5⅜ x 8.   T499 Paperbound **$1.25**

SYMBOLIC LOGIC and THE GAME OF LOGIC, Lewis Carroll. Two delightful puzzle books by the author of "Alice," bound as one. Both works concern the symbolic representation of traditional logic and together contain more than 500 ingenious, amusing and instructive syllogistic puzzlers. Total of 326pp. 5⅜ x 8.   T492 Paperbound **$1.50**

PILLOW PROBLEMS and A TANGLED TALE, Lewis Carroll. Two of Carroll's rare puzzle works bound as one. "Pillow Problems" contain 72 original math puzzles. The puzzles in "A Tangled Tale" are given in delightful story form. Total of 291pp. 5⅜ x 8.   T493 Paperbound **$1.50**

PECK'S BAD BOY AND HIS PA, G. W. Peck. Both volumes of one of the most widely read of all American humor books. A classic of American folk humor, also invaluable as a portrait of an age. 100 original illustrations. Introduction by E. Bleiler. 347pp. 5⅜ x 8.
                                                             T497 Paperbound **$1.35**

Dover publishes books on art, music, philosophy, literature, languages, history, social sciences, psychology, handcrafts, orientalia, puzzles and entertainments, chess, pets and gardens, books explaining science, intermediate and higher mathematics mathematical physics, engineering, biological sciences, earth sciences, classics of science, etc. Write to:

    Dept. catrr.
    Dover Publications, Inc.
    180 Varick Street, N. Y. 14, N. Y.